AF413170

Find Your Flow

Life is a journey of discovery.

Sometimes the wind blows in a direction that leads us away from our original objective.

Most of the time, it's "Our own damn fault".

Scream and shout.

Figure it out,

but

paddle back out.

Your wave is coming.

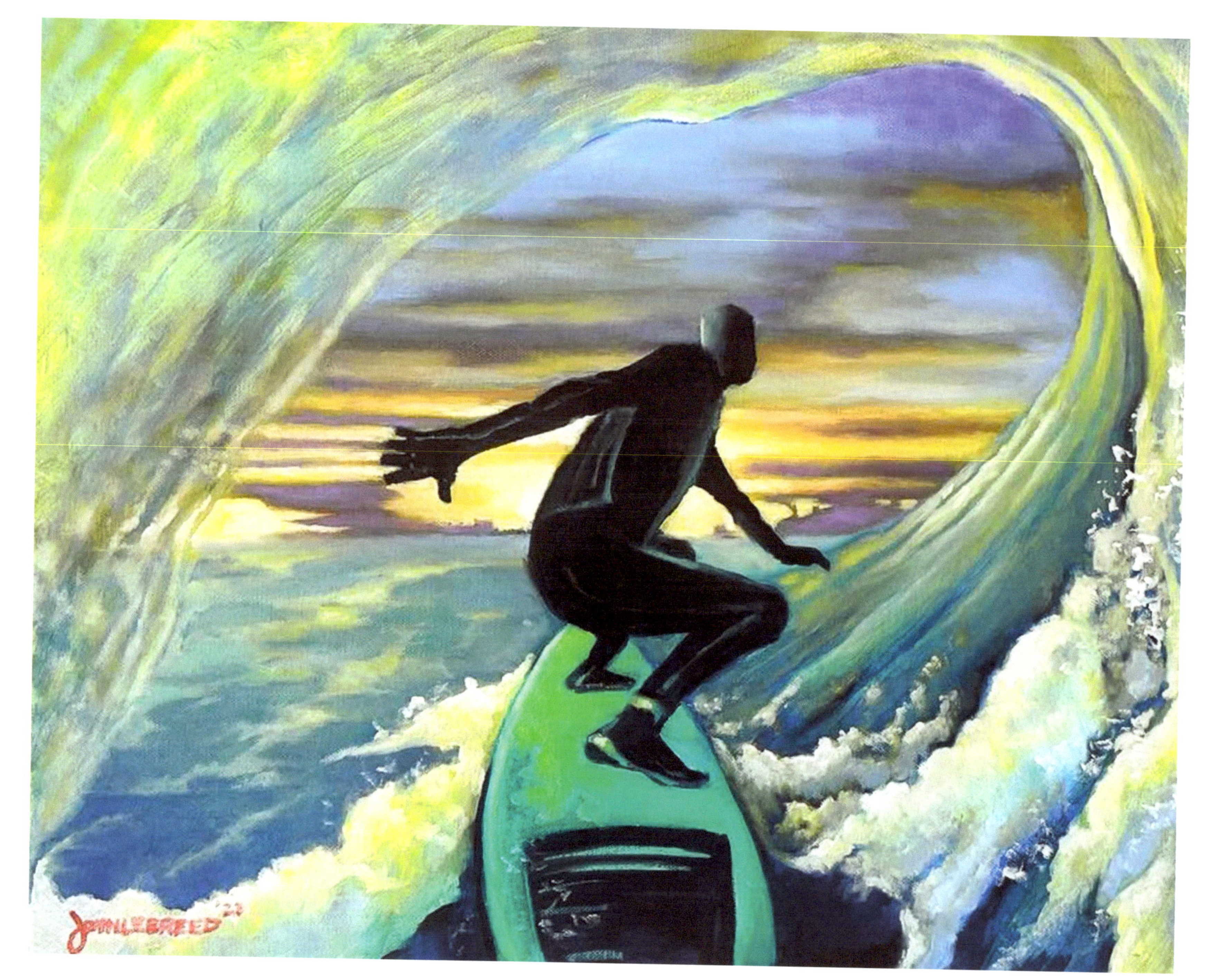

"Right Outta da Barrell" Oil on Canvas (Photo Ref. D. Neff)

Now, I ain't no Southern Preacher

and I surely ain't no Saint,

but if you'll read on just a little,

you just might smell the paint.

And when that permeation sets in

you'll come to understand,

the flow of your existence,

rests there in your own hands.

Life is for Learning

Ever feel like you are just cruising along in the dark?

Ever ask yourself – "After a lifetime of going to work, will I be satisfied with all that I've accomplished?"

Did I make the right choices and, most importantly…

Did I maximize my God-Given abilities? Was I true to the person I was meant to be?"

I don't know about you, but those are the questions that haunted me throughout my younger days and into my early working years.

I was always the kid who could draw.

 I drew and painted on every scrap of paper I could get my hands on. I plastered the walls of my bedroom with well-designed collages of my favorite sports figures, and I was continually in trouble for drawing images all over my clothes, shoes, and schoolbooks. In college, I even received an official 'Cease and Desist Order" from the Office of the Commandant at The Virginia Military Institute. It seemed that the Rock and Roll album covers (of which I intricately reproduced onto our newly issued, yellow uniform sweatshirts and sold by request to more than 40 different cadets) were deemed inappropriate for on-post, military and physical training.

Go figure.

My dad was also gifted creatively, and yet he had a relatively negative experience around the Creative Industries. By the time I reached college, I was told that I needed to put away those childish dreams of becoming an artist and focus on something that I could actually "make a living doing."

I knuckled under and got my History Degree.

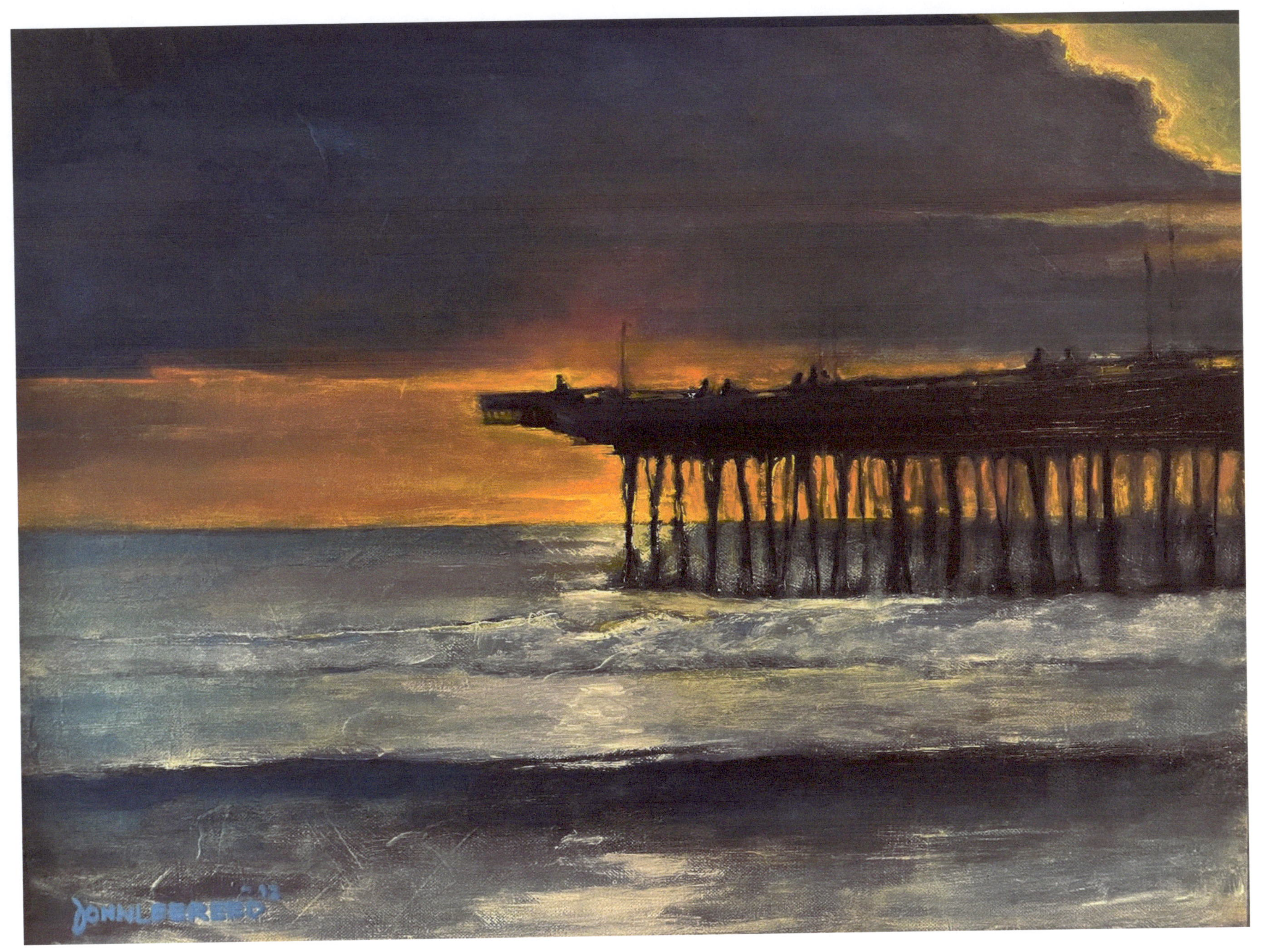

"Old Wooden Pier at Sunrise" Oil on Canvas

Sunrise at the Pier means only one thing 'Let's go surfing!"

Learning (Continued)

I entered the working world, trying to find a place where I could utilize my creative skills. I landed a job with a big advertising agency on Madison Avenue in New York City and figured I would be the next David Ogilvy (Google him). I felt like life had finally given me my big chance.

After a couple of years of getting my ass handed to me by guys and gals that were way smarter and better prepared than I was, I bailed before they had a chance to do it for me. I bounced around for a couple of years, more focused on my failures than on how I could find new success.

I needed to reexamine my perspective.

After failing my way to the last card in my hand, I was already approaching 30 years old. I had graduated from a respected, four-year military college but drowned in the deep end of the Madison Avenue advertising pool. On top of all that, I lost my right nut to a battle with testicular cancer. It was the bottom of the 9th, bases loaded with two outs, and I had two strikes on me. I knew full well the consequences of yet another swing and a miss.

One thing I have never lacked however, is self-confidence. I doubled down on myself. Against my dad's best advice, I borrowed a shit ton of money from the U.S. Government and drove down to Fort Lauderdale, Florida, to go to Art School.

I went on to be blessed with a successful 20+ year career as an award-winning Art Director and Creative Director. I almost killed myself searching for it, but I found my flow. Even then, as a commercial artist and designer, my job was to do the artwork that somebody ELSE wanted done. When I was finally able to emerge from the corporate world of commercial art and design, I vowed to create the art - that I wanted to create. It was then that I was truly swimming along with the

The flow of The Universe.

I hope you enjoy some of my favorite works. I'll try to share my motivations behind most of them along the way.

Charge on!

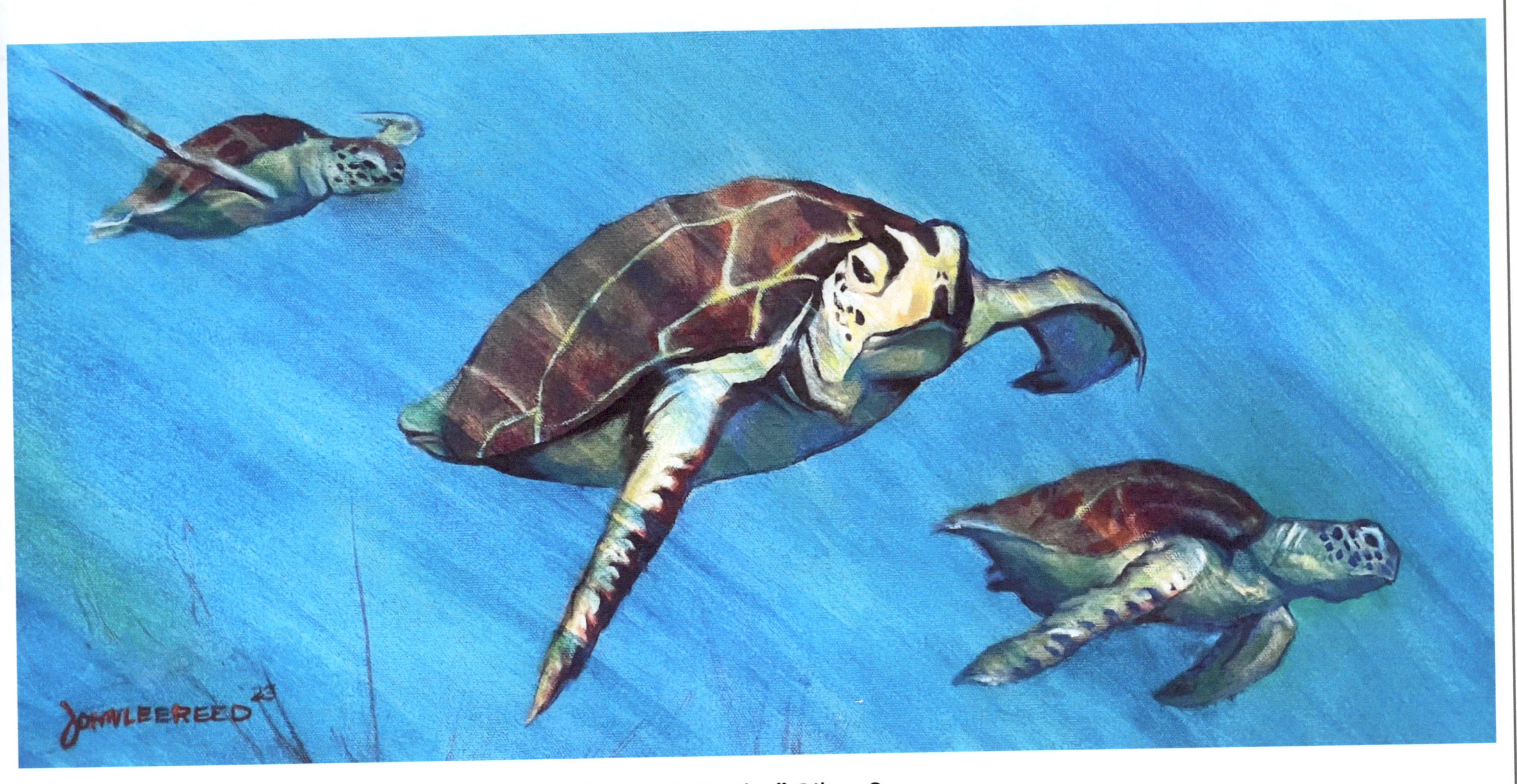

"LeeLee's Turtles" Oil on Canvas

Sea life, both in the water and on the water, has always been the primary focus of my creative energy. If you've had the chance to swim with these beautiful creatures, then you know how amazing they are. They live in the literal flow of the ocean, and we have a lot that we can learn from their peaceful and inquisitive nature.

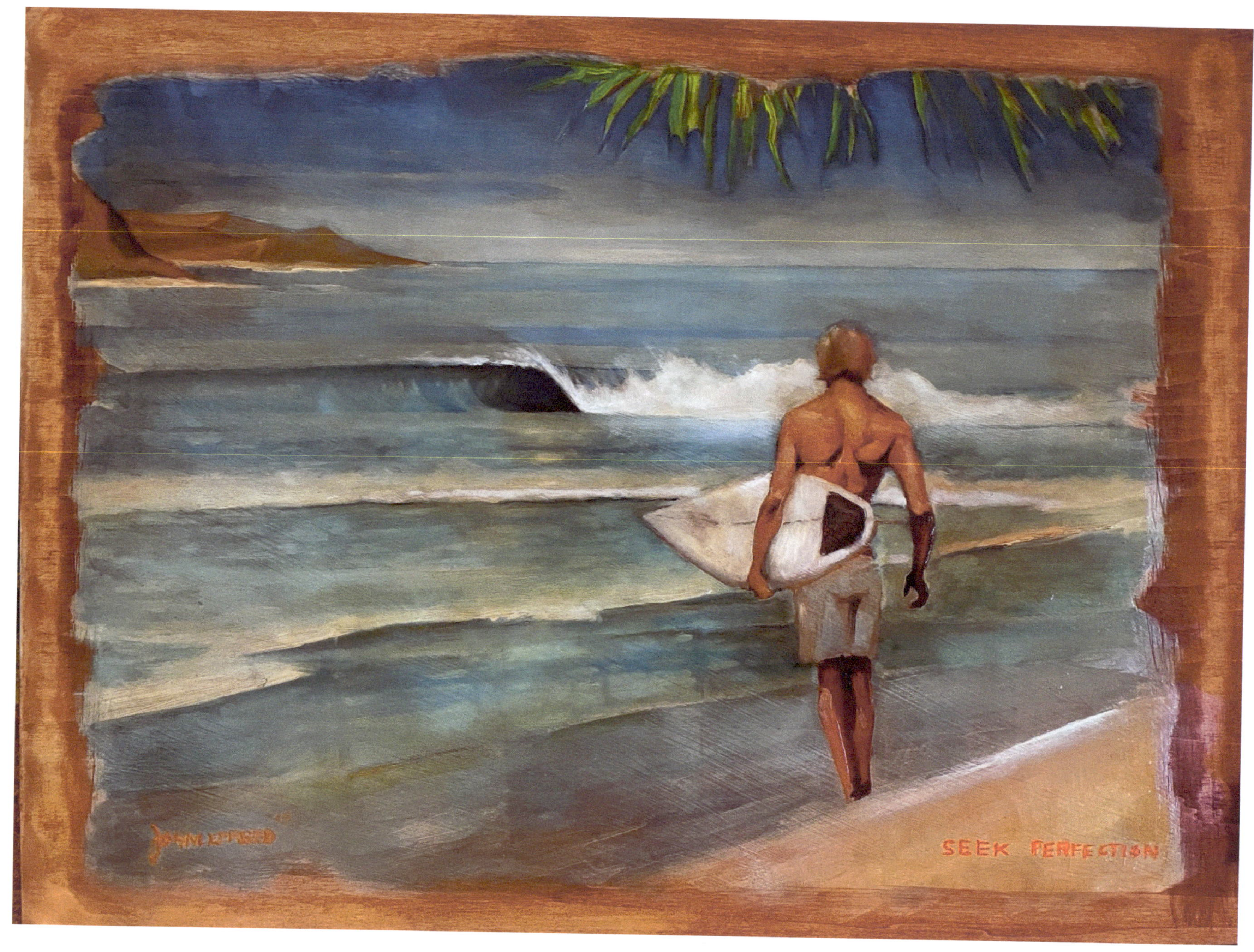

"Seek Perfection" Oil on Birch Panel

Goal #1 on the Surfer's Life Quadrant

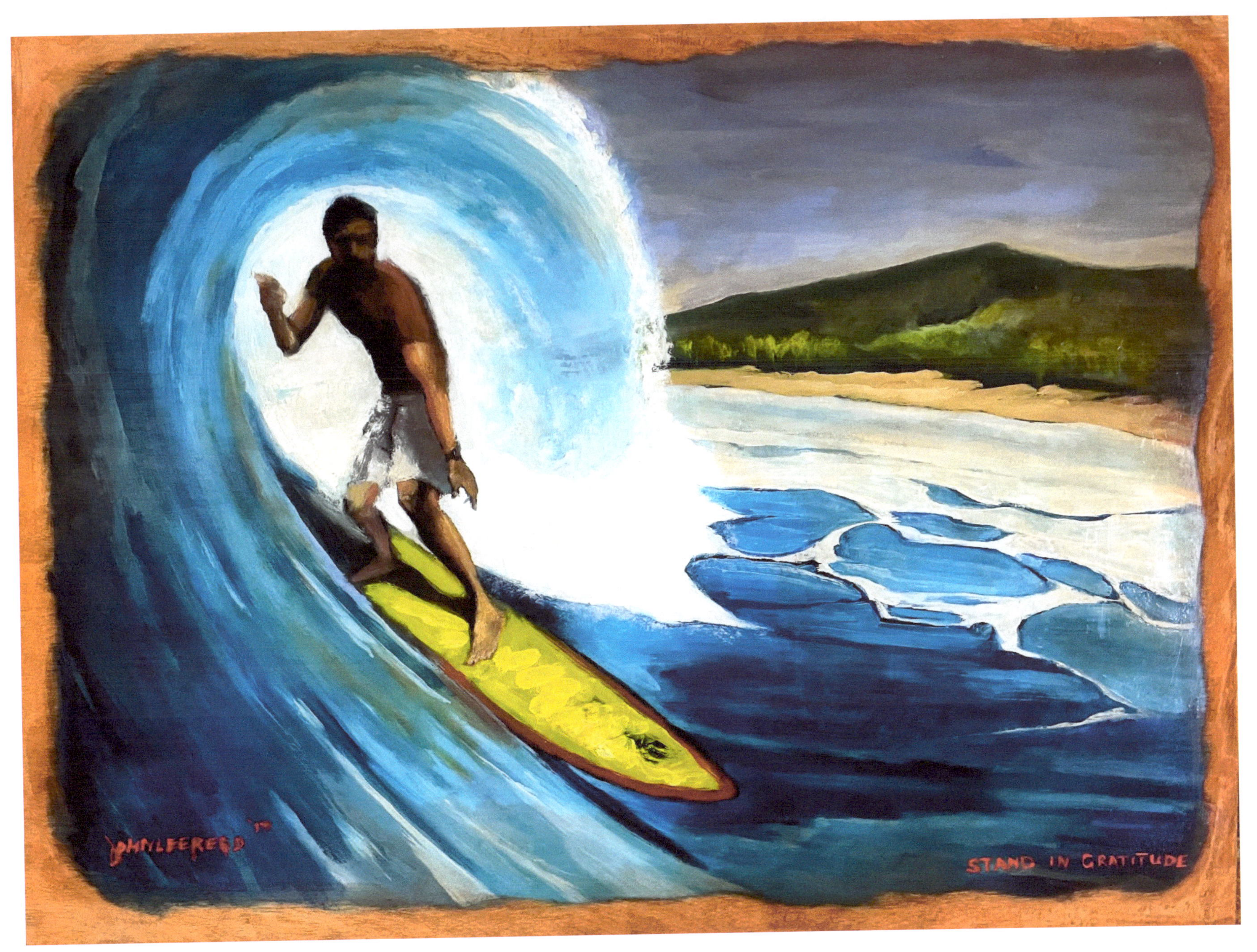

"Stand in Gratitude" Oil on Birch Panel

Goal #2 on the Surfer's Life Quadrant

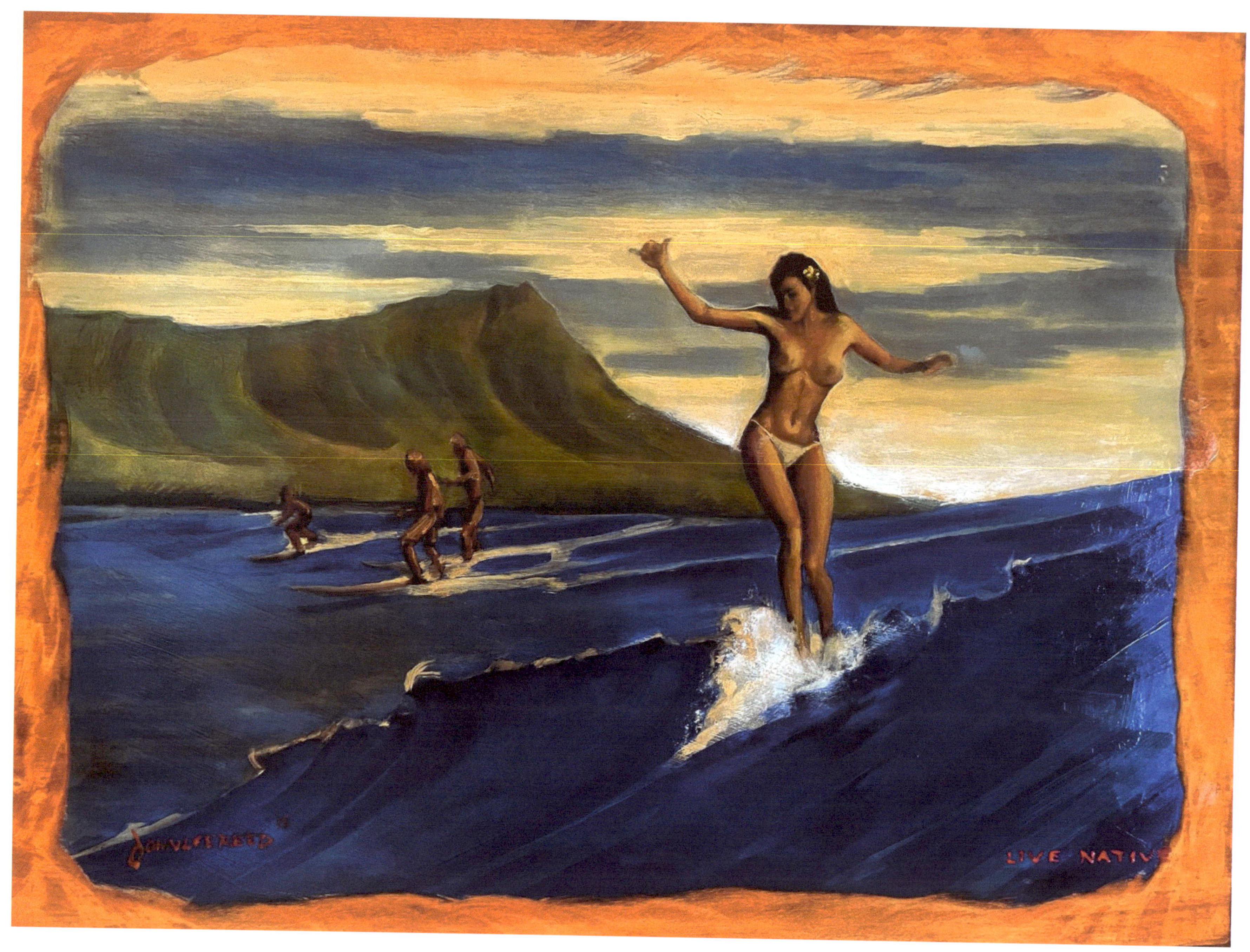

"Live Native" Oil on Birch Panel

Goal #3 on the Surfer's Life Quadrant

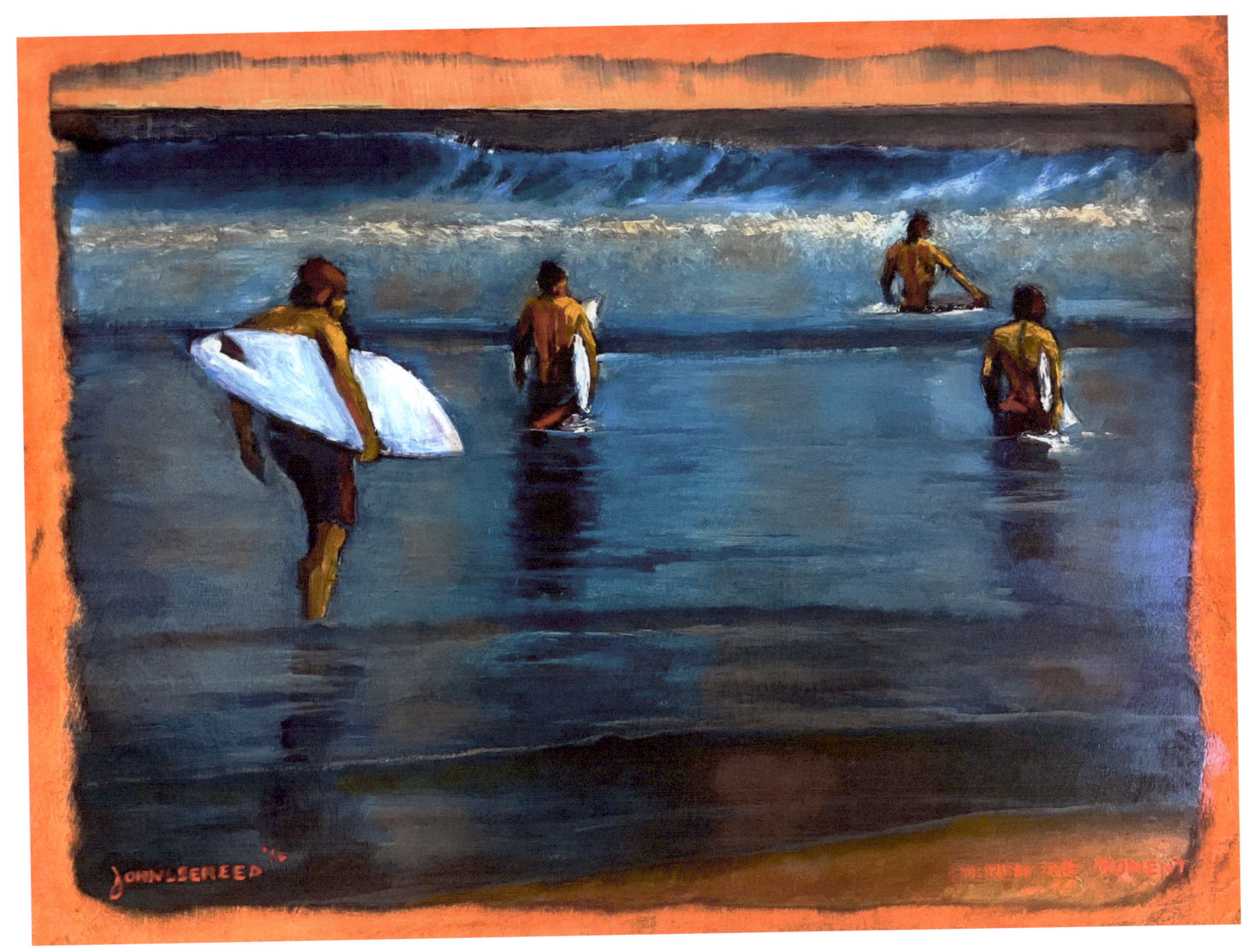

"Cherish the Moment" Oil on Birch Panel

Goal #4 on the Surfer's Life Quadrant

What is Your Life Quadrant?

Every game you play comes with a set of rules. The game of life is no different.

When I was working on Madison Avenue in the fast-paced world of national advertising, every brand we worked on had a Creative Objective. That concise objective was written out and signed off on by every member of the marketing team and was always referred to as the defining principle for every decision we made. Throughout my career as a Creative Director, I always made sure that in every endeavor, we had a clear, well-defined Creative Objective to follow.

As we venture through this book together, I may refer to the **"Surfer"** as a seemingly ethereal and even mythical character with a sublime consciousness to which you and I may only strive to achieve.

Are all surfers such animals? Maybe not, but the pure act of paddling out into a dynamic ocean in search of sliding down the face of a breaking wave requires a singular focus that brings out the best in anyone who attempts such a feat. Whether you are Kelly Slater or just a long-board cruiser, surfing in all its forms is an attempt to better harmonize the human spirit with The Universe in which we have been temporarily assigned.

But why a Quadrant?

The Quadrant was used by sailors and early explorers dating back to the Age of Exploration in the early 1400s. In their case, the Quadrant was one-fourth of a full circle designed to measure the height of Polaris, the Pole star. Astrologers would use the Quadrant to help determine an eclipse of the sun or to forecast someone's fate with help from the stars. It was simply a device for measuring the angular height of any star.

A few years later, Andy Warhol set the art world on its ear by using the Quadrant to highlight iconic images screened by contrasting and complimentary colors. If you study the psychology of art, you'll find the human brain is attracted to this symmetrical breakdown.

The Surfer's Quadrant is simply a set of easy, concise goals to follow, in an effort to obtain a certain objective; just like a Creative Objective.

In this case, it is designed to keep the focus on the amazing blessings offered to us as we go through the game of life,

Surfing the Universe.

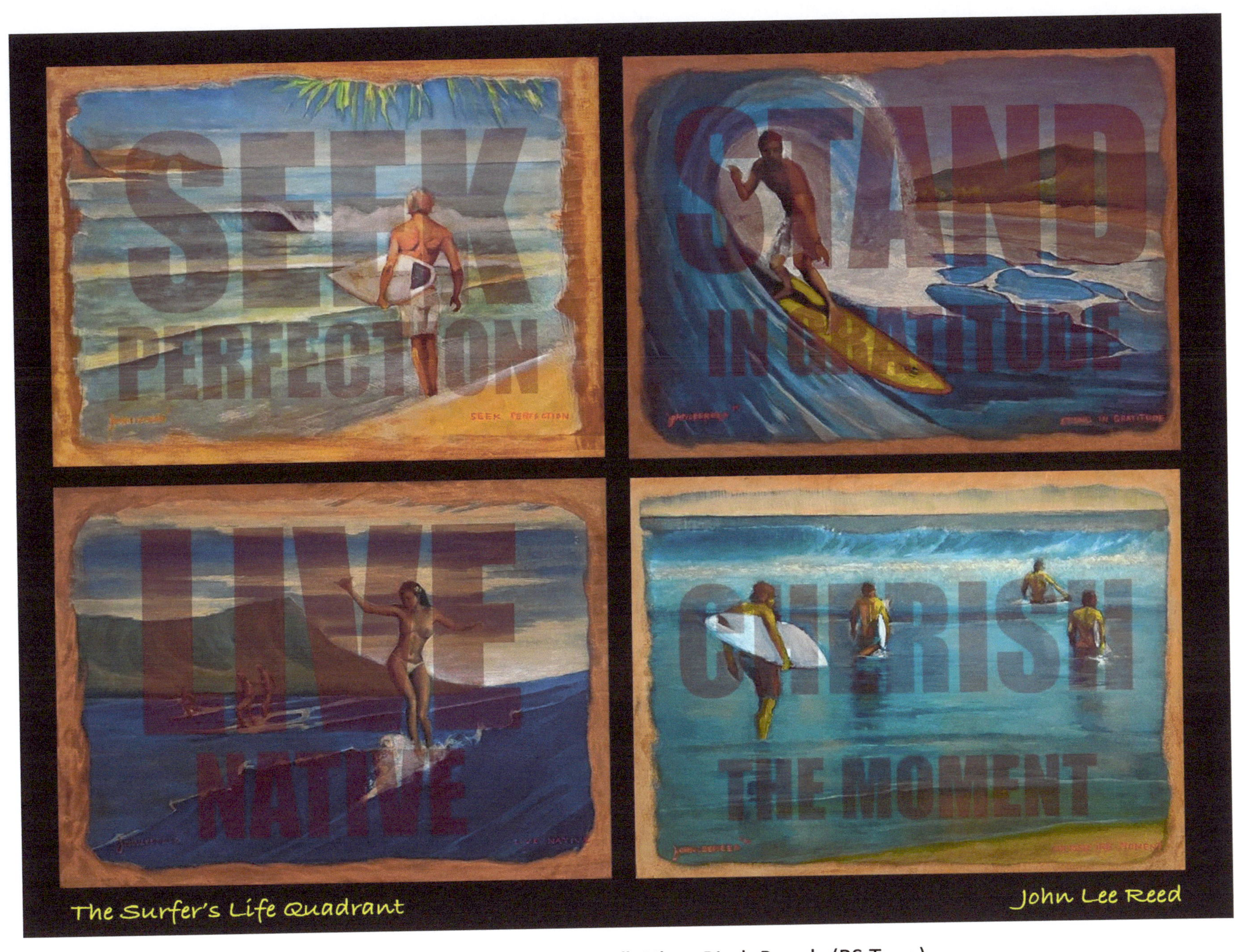

"The Surfer's Life Quadrant" Oil on Birch Panels (PS Type)

Seek Perfection, Stand in Gratitude, Live Native, and Cherish the Moment. The four quadrants balance out a surfer's life.

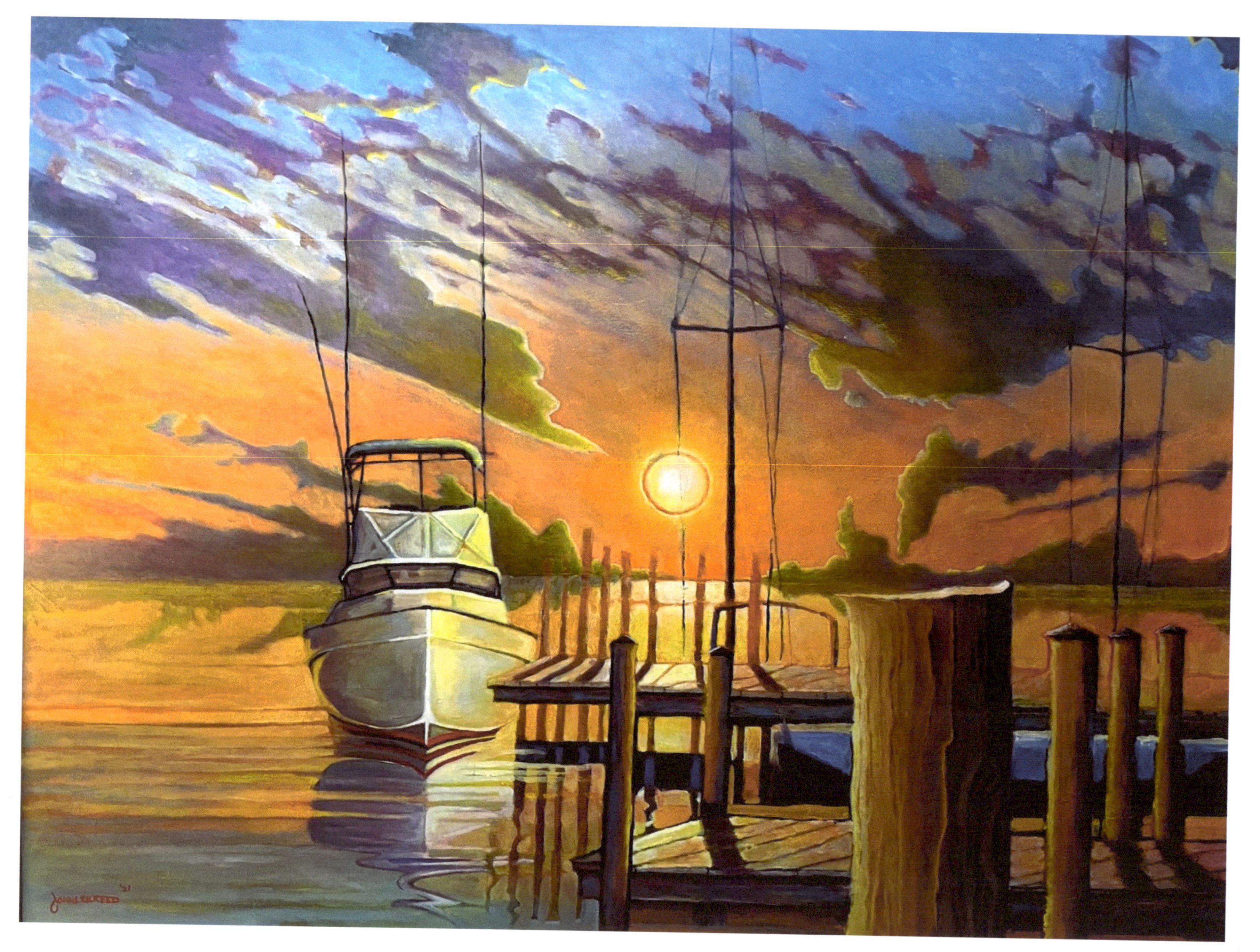

"Backyard of Dreams" Oil on Canvas

I fell in love with the water at an early age and was lucky enough to experience it in all its glory.

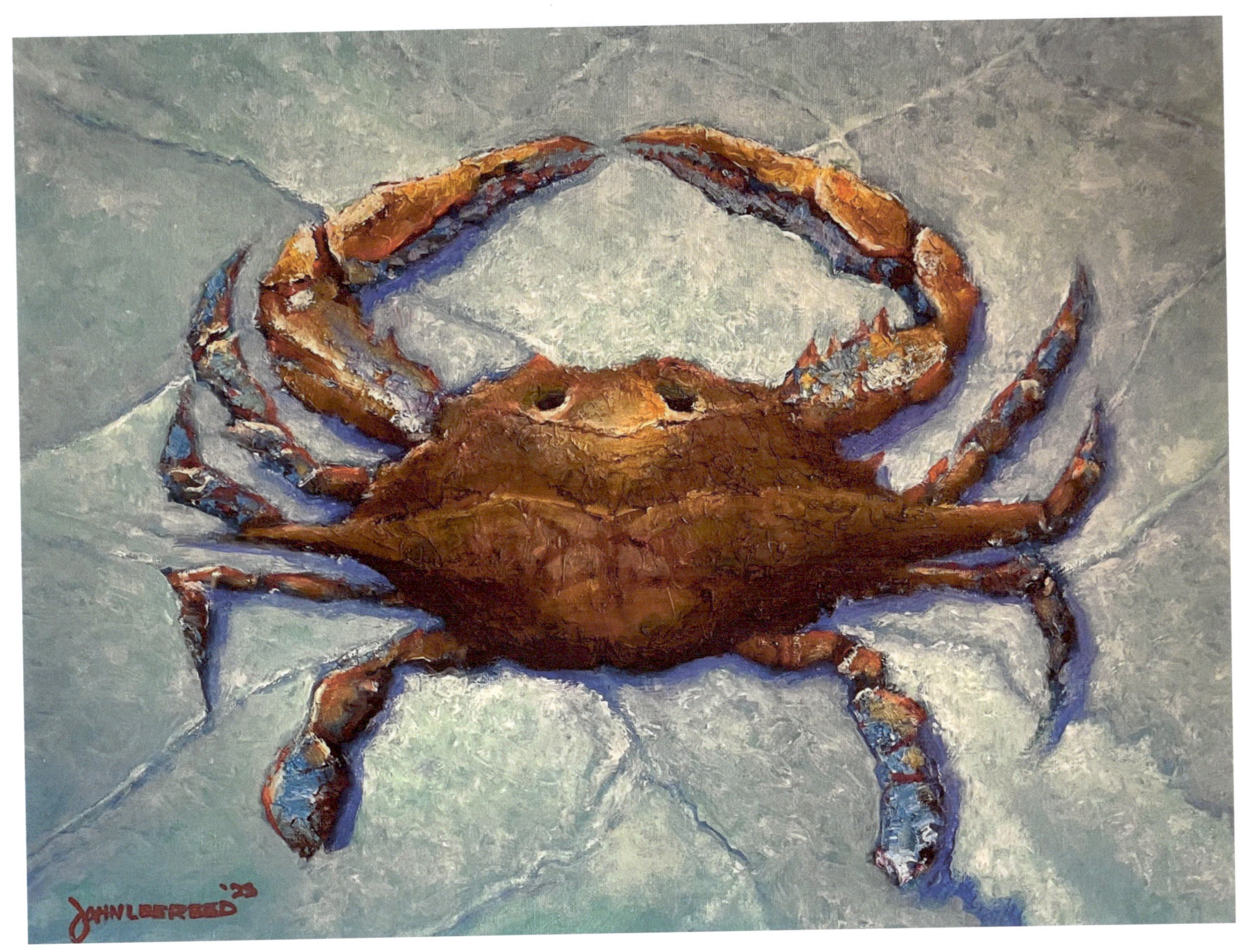

"Jimmy Blue" Oil on Canvas

The Ocean's bounty is incredible. Living on the Chesapeake Bay, we found ourselves alongside an abundance of wonderful (and tasty) creatures that our environment allowed us to share.

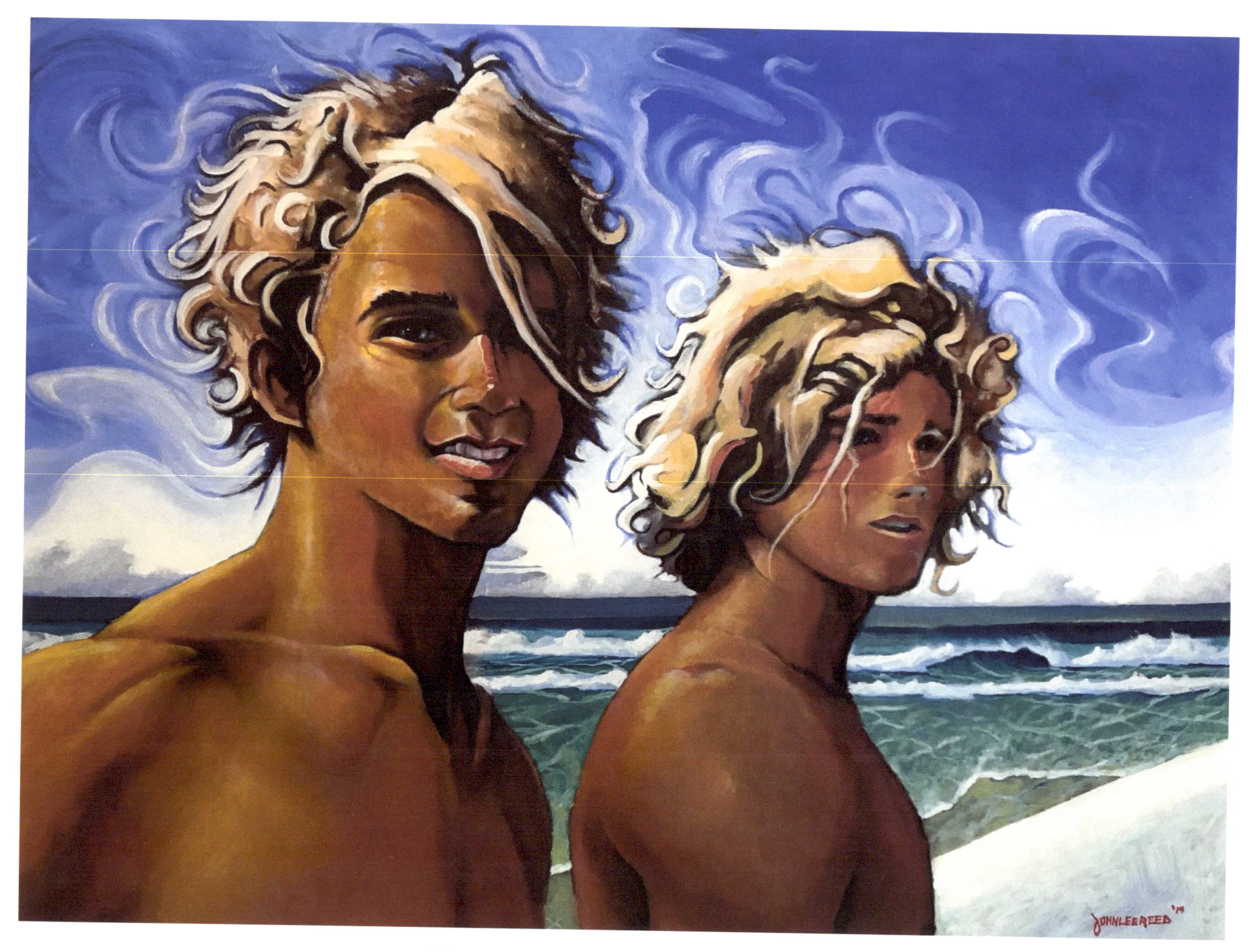

"The Boys of Summer" Oil on Canvas

Growing up, we spent our days on the beaches of Virginia and North Carolina. We had the "bushy-bushy, blonde hairdos," sunburns from April Fool's Day to Halloween, and saltwater unexpectedly gushing from our sinuses whenever we sat still for even a second.

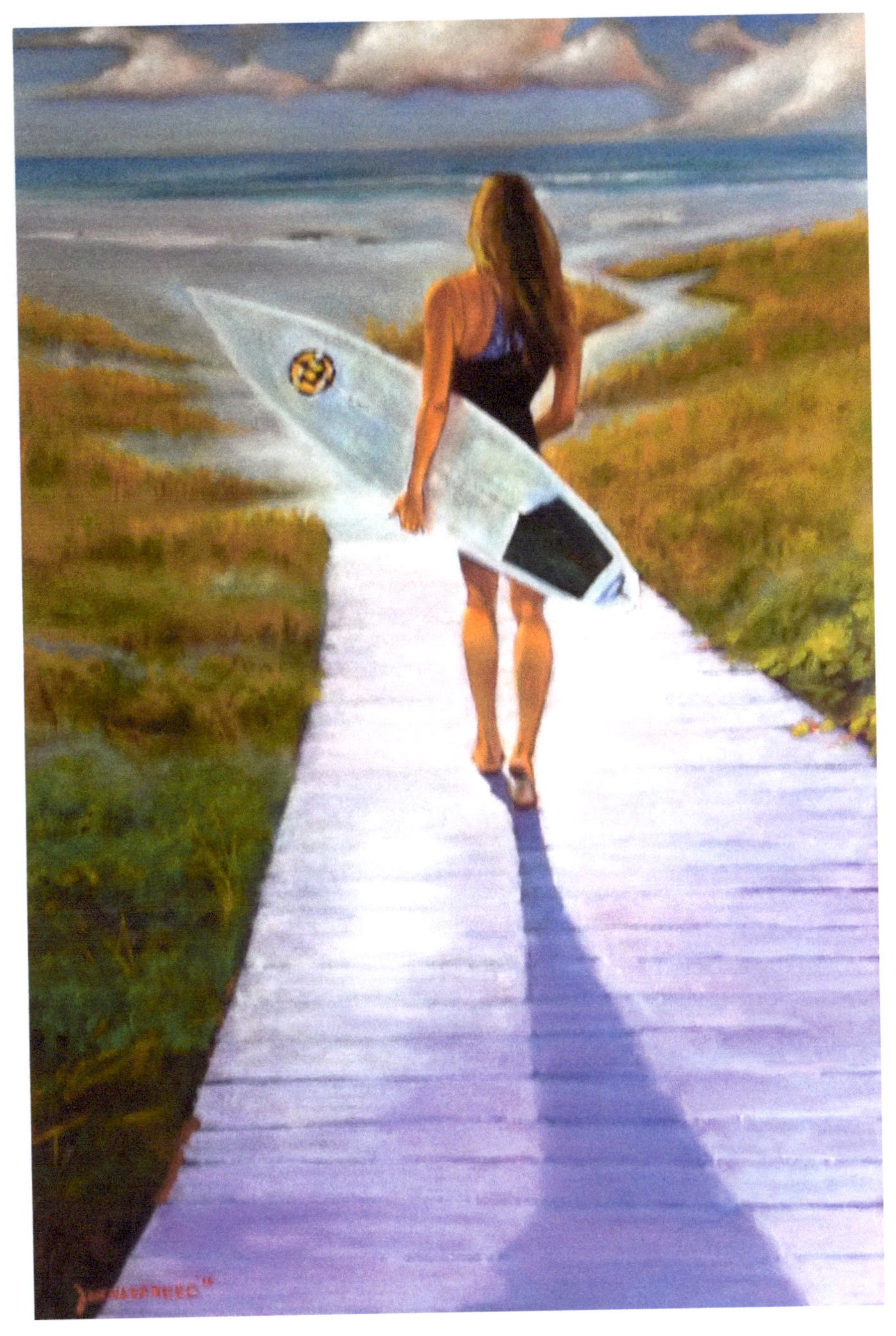

"Kate Charging the Day" Oil on Birch Panel

It was never just the boys dropping in to enjoy a day of surfing. In VB everyone hit the beach for all it had to offer.

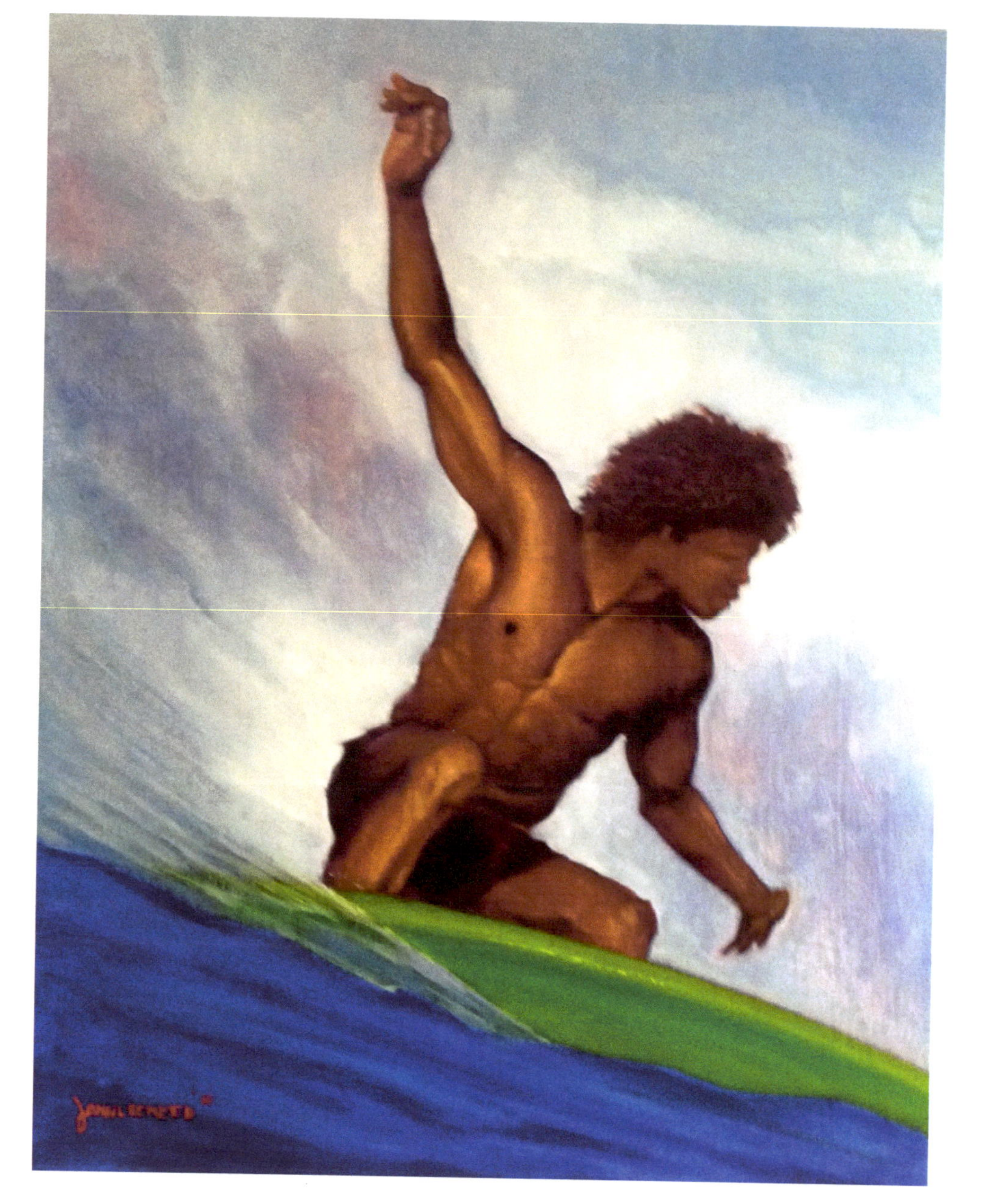

"70's Style" Oil on Birch Panel

As kids, we devoured SURFER magazine to read about the Hawaiian surfers who were changing the dynamic of the sport. We packed the local FOP Club halls when new surf films came out and hooted and hollered at the fluid movements of our idols riding the big waves we rarely got to see. It seemed like a dream to be able to surf Hawaii, California and other far away destinations.

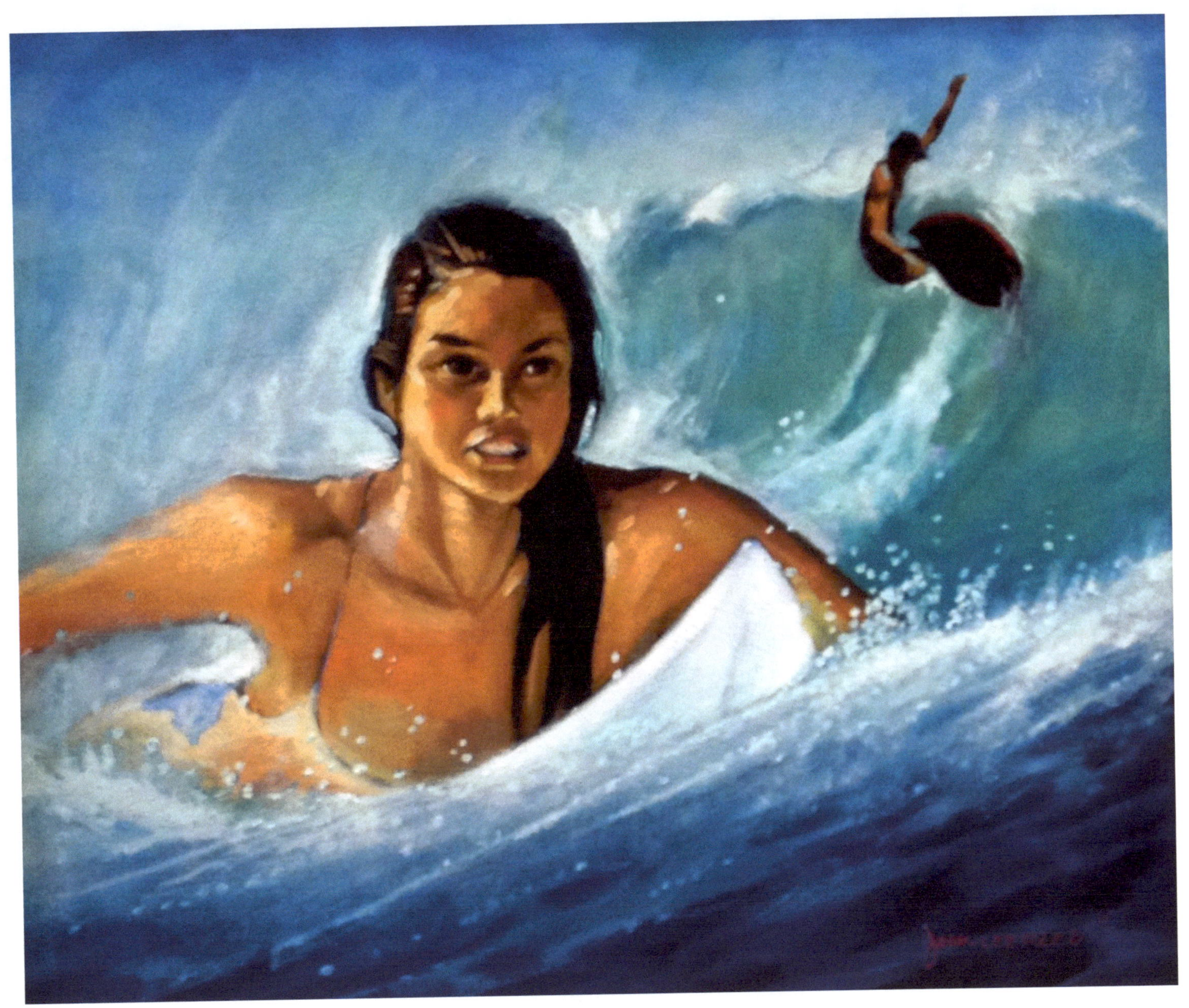

"Alamo Now & Then" Oil on Canvas

I did this piece to honor our heroes from 70's surfing and contrast them with the stars of today's sport. This image refers back to John Severson's classic shot of Gerry Lopez off the wall in Ala Moana. It hung in the gallery for a time at the Surfing Heritage and Cultural Museum in San Clemente, CA.

Our True Heroes

Hawaiian surfers, NFL and NBA athletes, young, good-looking tennis and golf champions, professional coaches, and action movie stars: That's who we looked up to when we were kids. Those were the people that we thought we needed to emulate and pattern our lives after.

Such is the thinking of those with but a few decades of perspective.

Our true heroes however, were (literally) right there in our own backyards. The problem was that they were trying to make responsible adults out of us when all we wanted to do was - have a little fun! It's kind of hard sometimes to idolize a person when they are always on your butt about cleaning out the gutters or getting your homework done. They were there, however, and after becoming a father myself, I came to understand that is the single most important thing you can do.

Plain and simple, the kids in my generation were the recipients of the greatness that our parents' generation created for us.

After getting a few years under my belt and coming to understand what great role models we had right there in our own lives, I wanted to show my appreciation in any way that I could. I was lucky enough to be able to paint the portraits of several of my local role models.

Captain Tom McClenahan is a decorated naval aviator, Squadron, and E-2 Wing Commander. He also just happened to be the father of one of my best friends growing up in Virginia Beach. I'll always respect Tom's calm, sensible demeanor and his delightful sense of humor. I painted his portrait from a photograph given to me by his son, and I added my own flag background to highlight those dashing navy whites.

William "Bill" McIntosh was also the father of a friend of mine growing up. Bill was an award-winning photographer who built a dynamic company with his creative skills and business savvy. He was a great inspirational figure for me growing up because he was the first person I ever knew who made a career out of his artistic ability. I painted Bill's portrait for his daughter, who has been a longtime friend.

Captain William Span was yet another father of friends of mine growing up. The dashing and dynamic Naval Jet Fighter Pilot flew hundreds of missions over Viet Nam and was the first American pilot to fly the Russian MIG. As kids, we did a lot of hunting and fishing with their family, and I was honored to get to paint Bill's portrait and give it to him before he passed away.

Just goes to show you that sometimes your heroes can be closer to you than you might think.

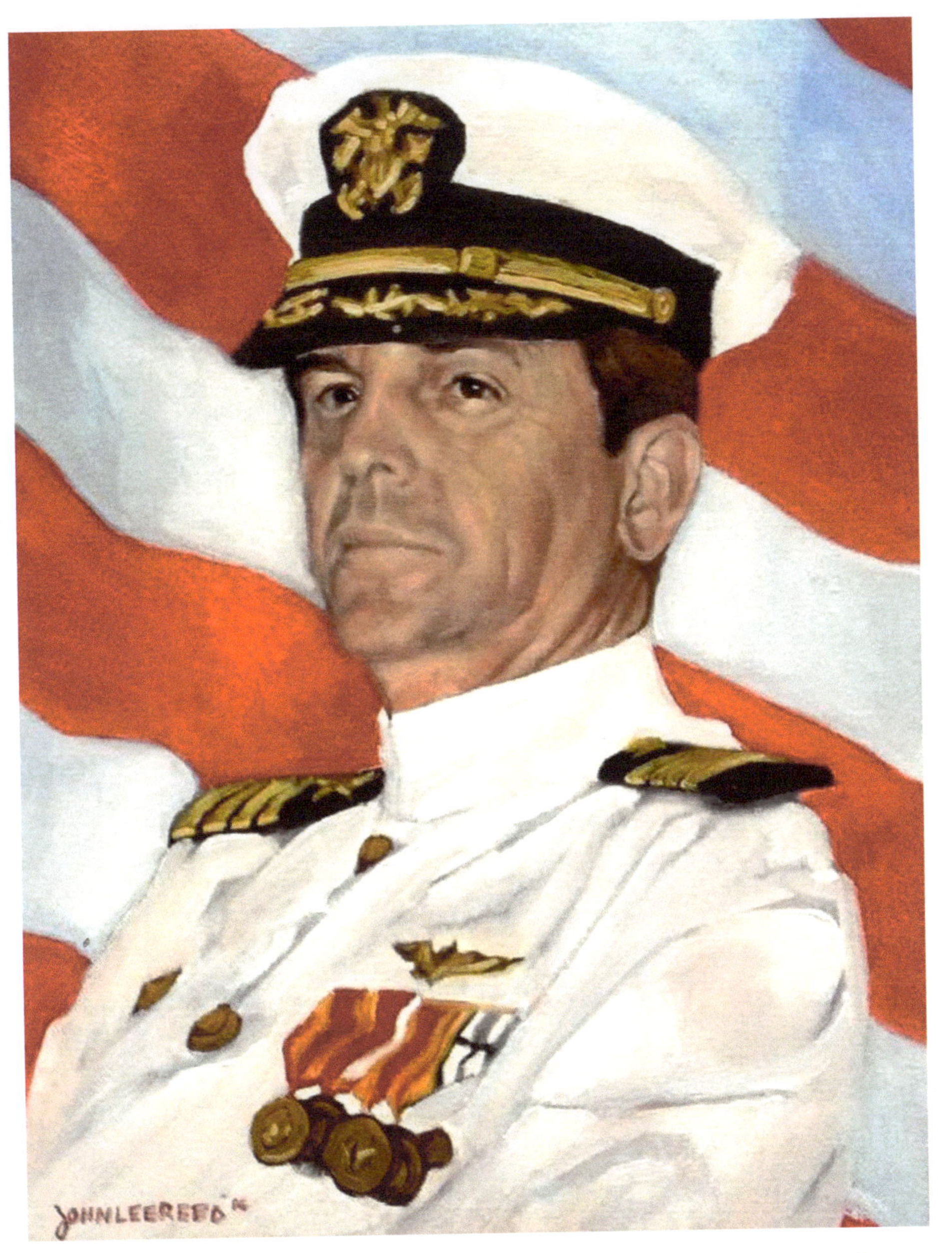

"Captain McClenahan" Oil on Canvas

Many of the kids I grew up with were from Navy families stationed in Norfolk and Virginia Beach. Over the years I've been lucky enough to paint a few of the distinguished naval officers that shaped our local character. Captain Tom McClenahan is one of my favorites.

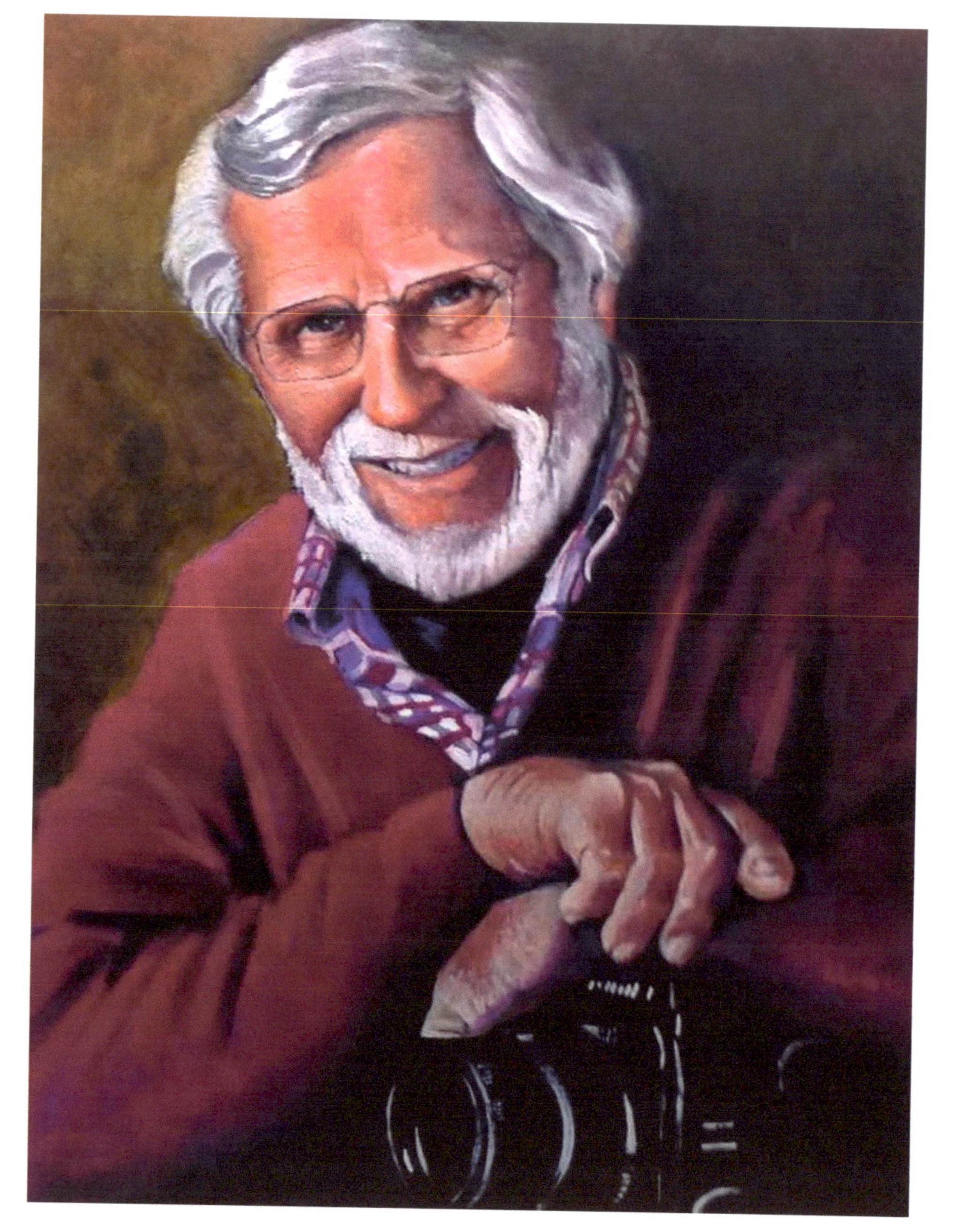

"Bill McIntosh" Oil on Canvas

A great photographer and a wonderful man, Bill showed me that you could find success in life by sharing your creative talent.

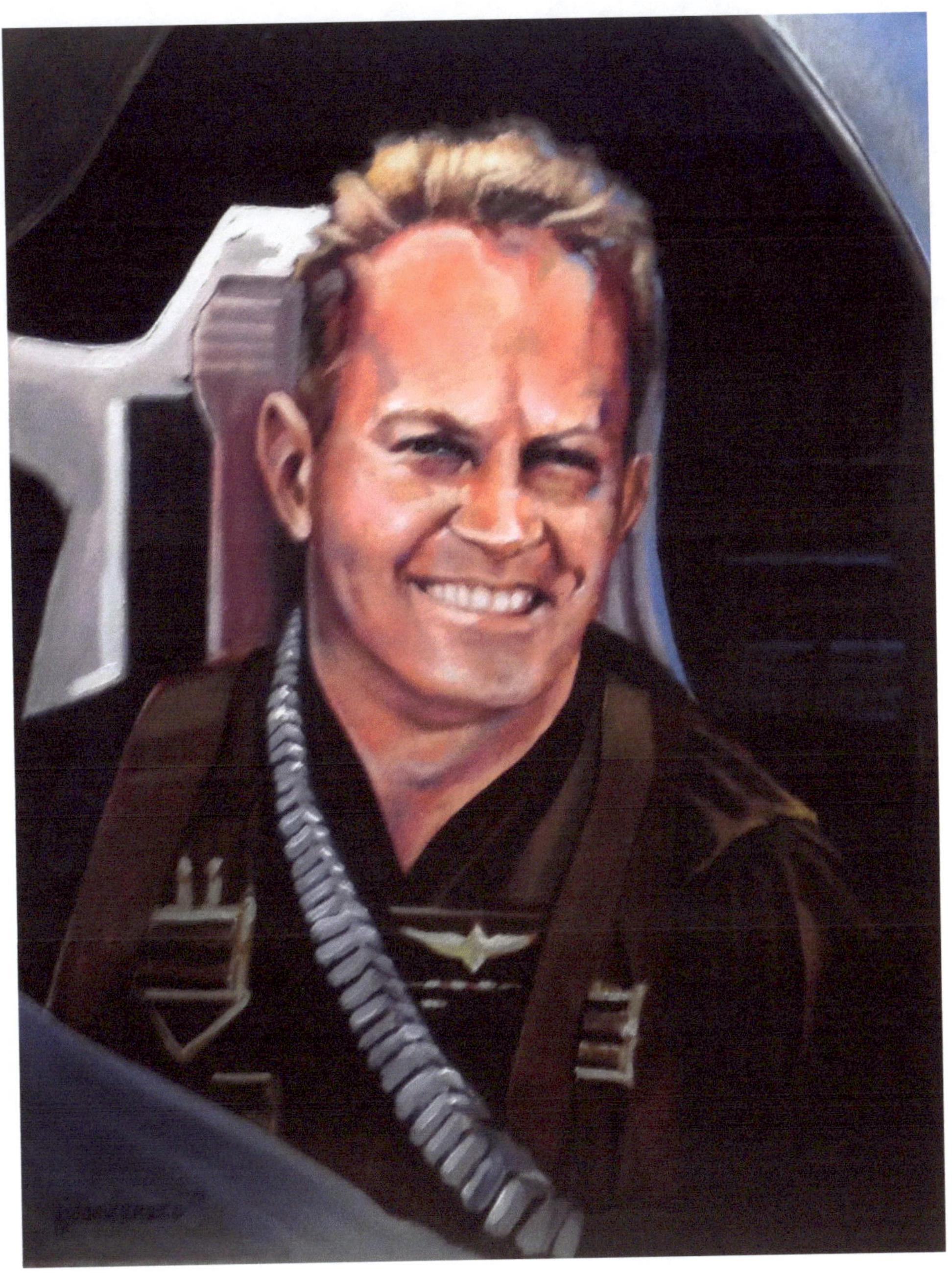

"Captain Bill Span" Oil on Canvas

A dynamic soldier, pilot, outdoorsman and father, Captain Span taught me that life could be a very exciting place, if only you are able to find a niche that uses your talents to keep you focused and challenged.

Recognize Your Navigational Beacons

As I said, I've been drawing and painting for as long as I can remember.

I'm sure I've surpassed that magic 10,000 hours that some say it takes to get "good" at any single, individual pursuit.

Personally, I'm still waiting to get "good."

(What the heck is so great about being "good" anyway?)

I once had an art instructor tell me that my paintings looked like I was "tripping on mushrooms."

"Cool. Thanks." I told her.

"Let me know if you ever want to paint together."

I wasn't always able to be that confident. In fact, for years, I struggled to find my way.

You've probably felt like that before. I know I'm not the only one who went through my 20s watching friends become uber-successful while I couldn't get off my bar stool long enough to figure out what I wanted to do with my life. Luckily, The Universe sent me several navigational beacons along my journey. I absolutely believe they were Angels. When I finally opened my eyes and began to recognize them, things in my life started to get better.

It wasn't until I had exhausted every option, and I was literally knocking on death's door, that I finally discovered my path.

My only insight for you, or anyone else on a journey of self-expression, is this:

The Universe loves you when you're creating!

Be sure to open your eyes and your heart to the beacons that It

provides for you along the way.

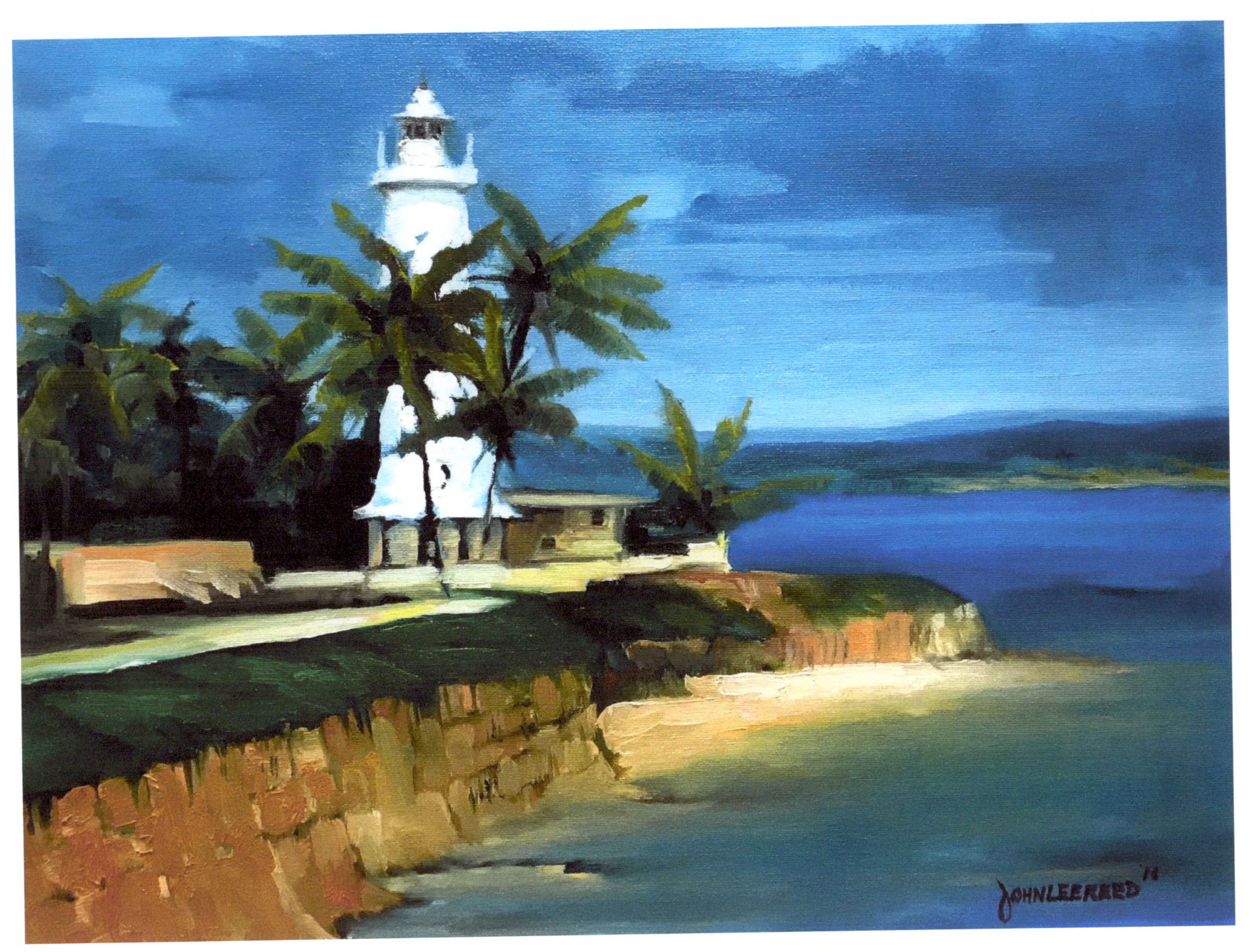

"Mediterranean Light" Oil on Canvas

Sometimes disguised, navigational beacons are essential for recognition as you travel the road of life.

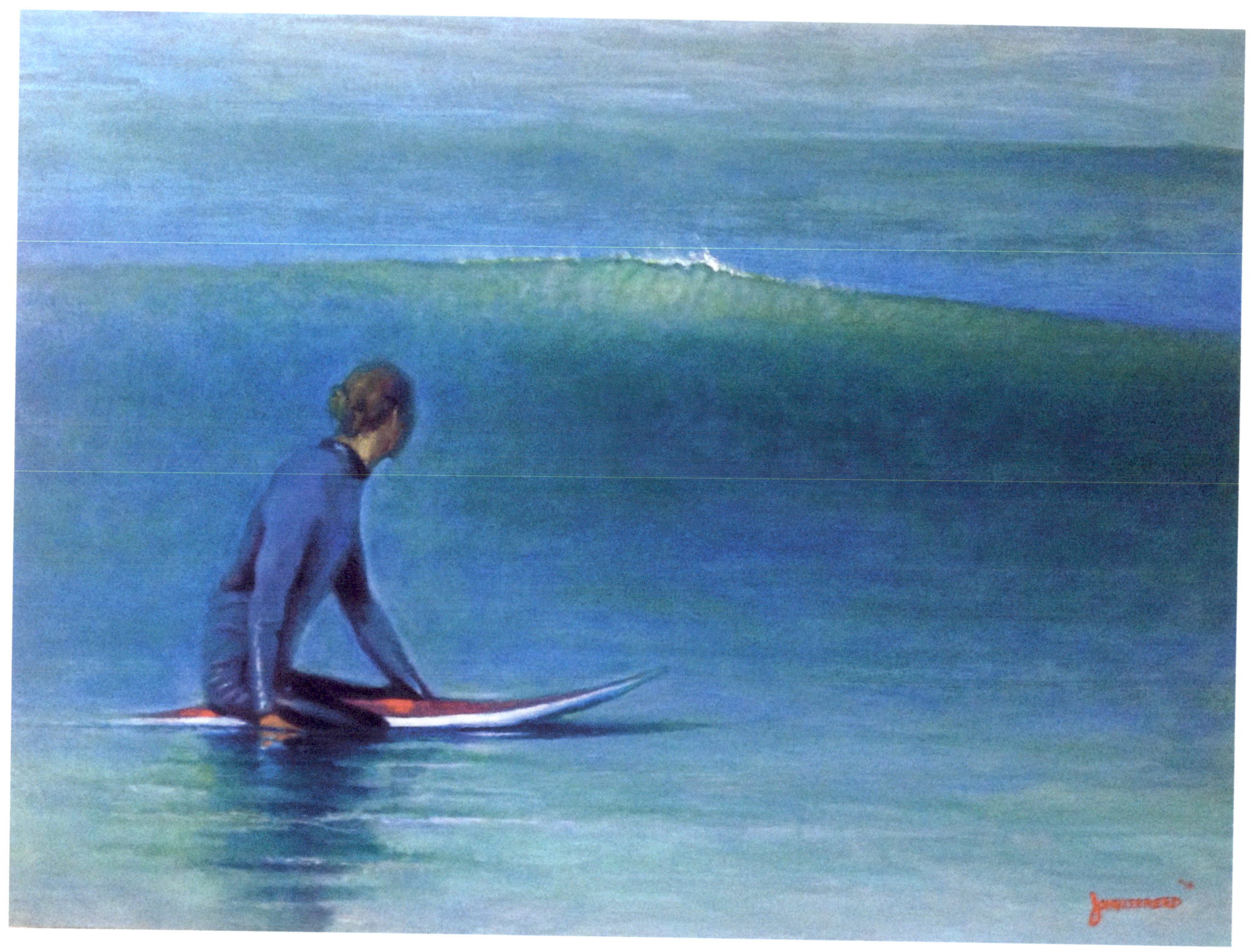

"Go Time" Oil on Canvas

When we weren't fishing on the Chesapeake Bay or chasing girls around Virginia Beach, we were usually surfing. Wintertime on the East Coast provided the best waves, and when the swell was up, it was Go time!

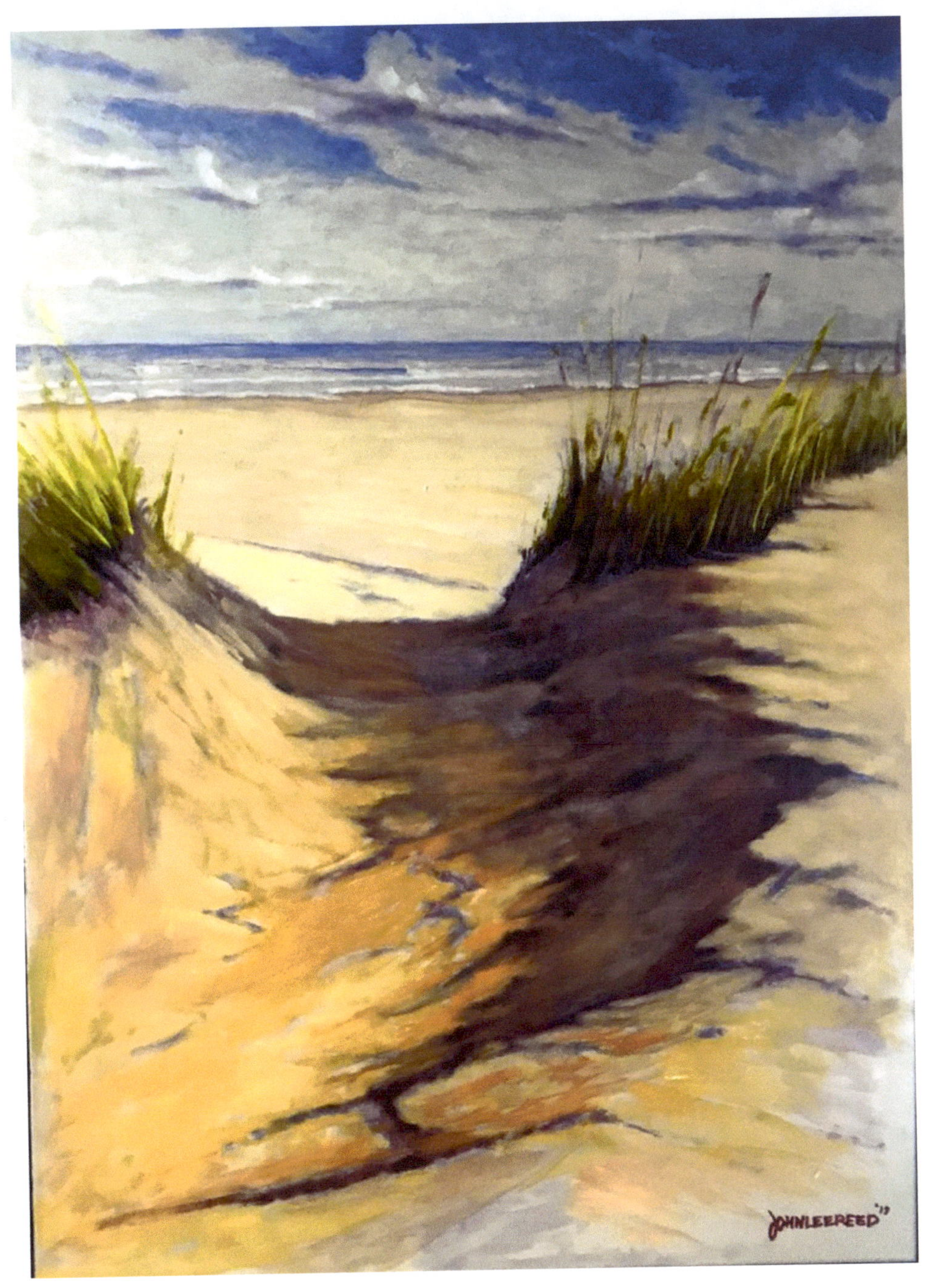

"Secret Spot" Oil on Canvas

Most of our favorite beaches had secret surf breaks that were only known to the locals.

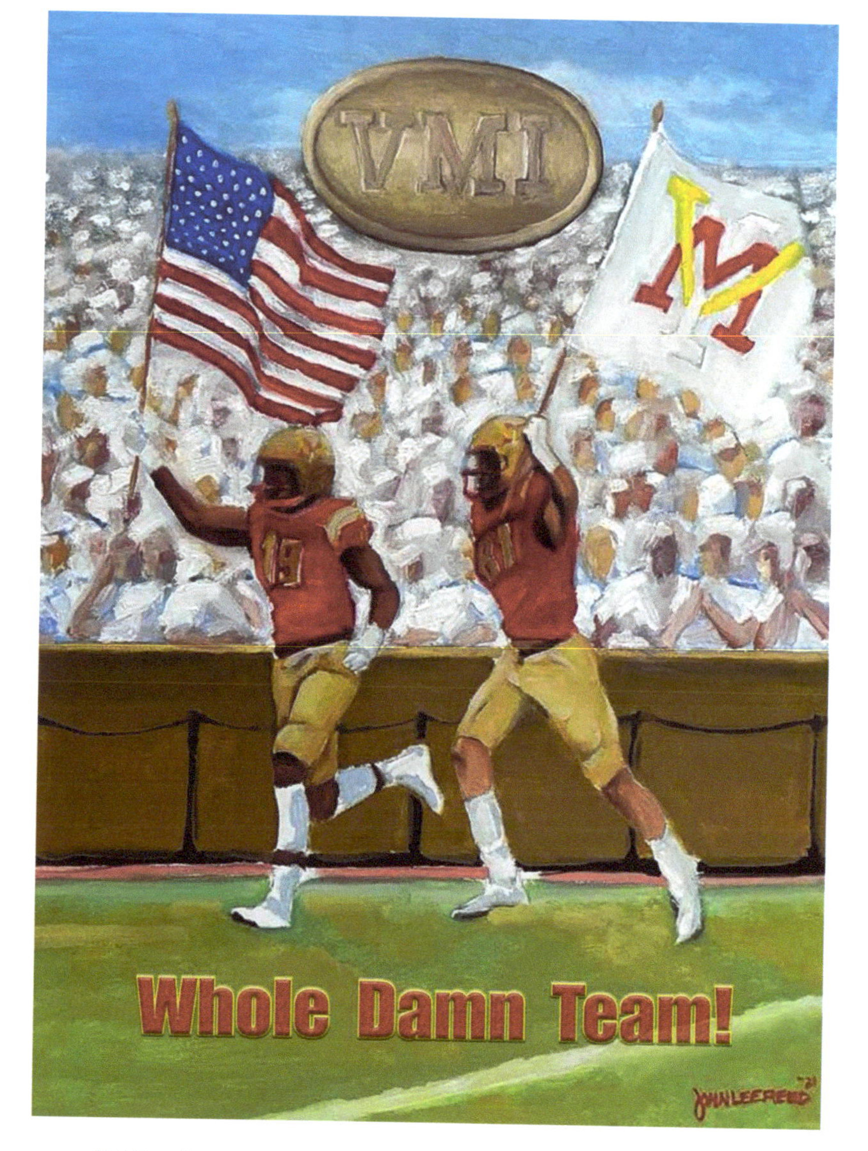

"Whole Damn Team" Oil on Canvas (PS Type)

Football was (and still is) my first true love. When I was 17, I wanted nothing more than to play Division I College Football. I got that opportunity at The Virginia Military Institute where I was a wide receiver for two seasons and aptly labeled an "Average White Boy". Like a lot of my early ventures football didn't quite live up to my lofty expectations, but it was still an experience that I wouldn't trade for the world. I think most athletes will tell you, the relationships made through sports last a lifetime.

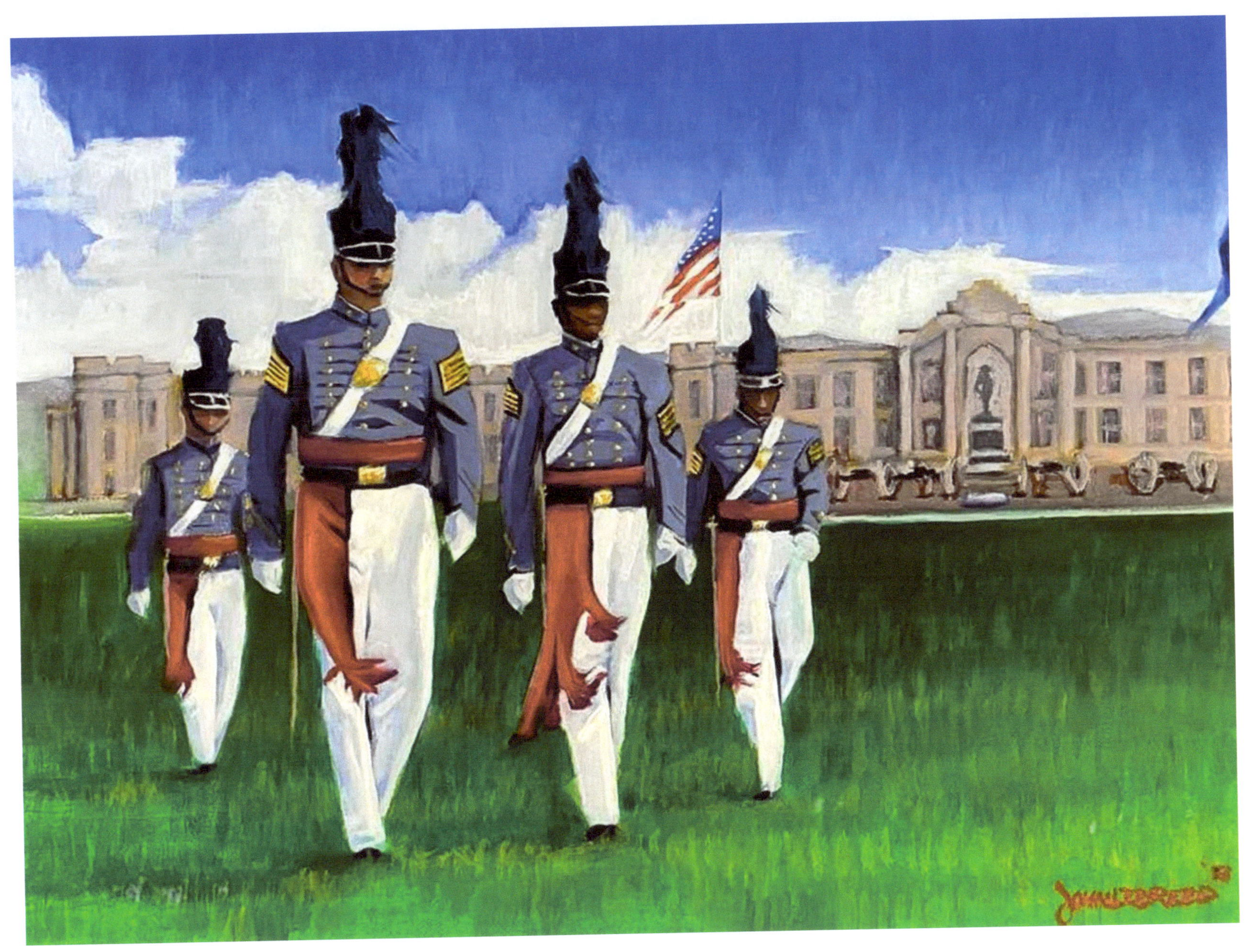

"Let the Parade Begin" Oil on Canvas

My dad and I both knew that I needed a "structured environment" if I was ever going to make it through college. VMI invited me to come play football for them, and that was all it took. It ended up being one of the proudest accomplishments of my life.

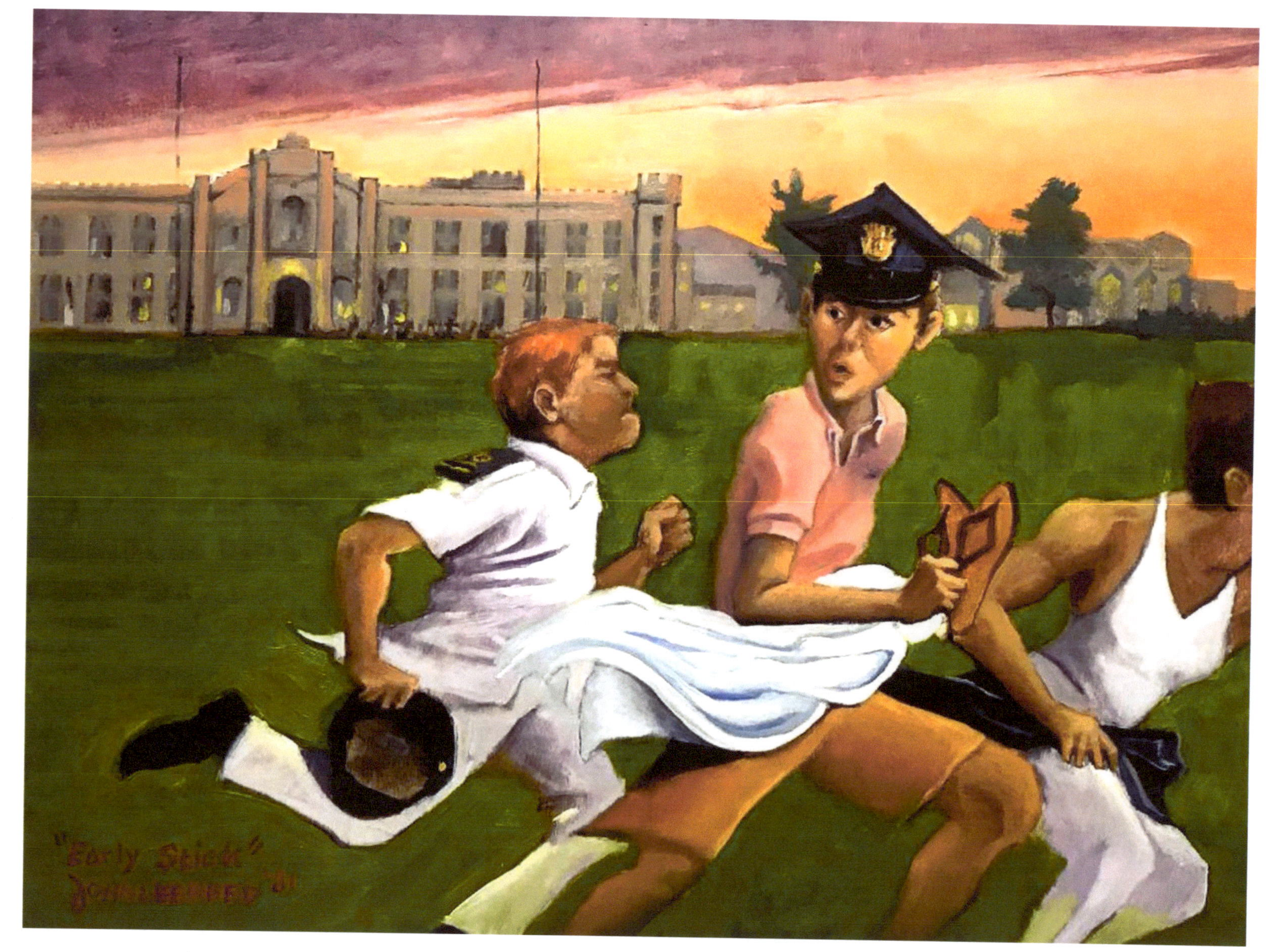

"Early Stick" Oil on Birch Panel

This fun, little painting was inspired by Norman Rockwell's famous 1921 Saturday Evening Post cover titled "No Swimming." We had a lot of innocent fun at The Institute, pushing the limits of the rules just a bit. Unless you attended VMI or one of the service academies, you probably won't "get" what this painting is about. If you know someone who did, however, I guarantee you that you are in for a funny story or two.

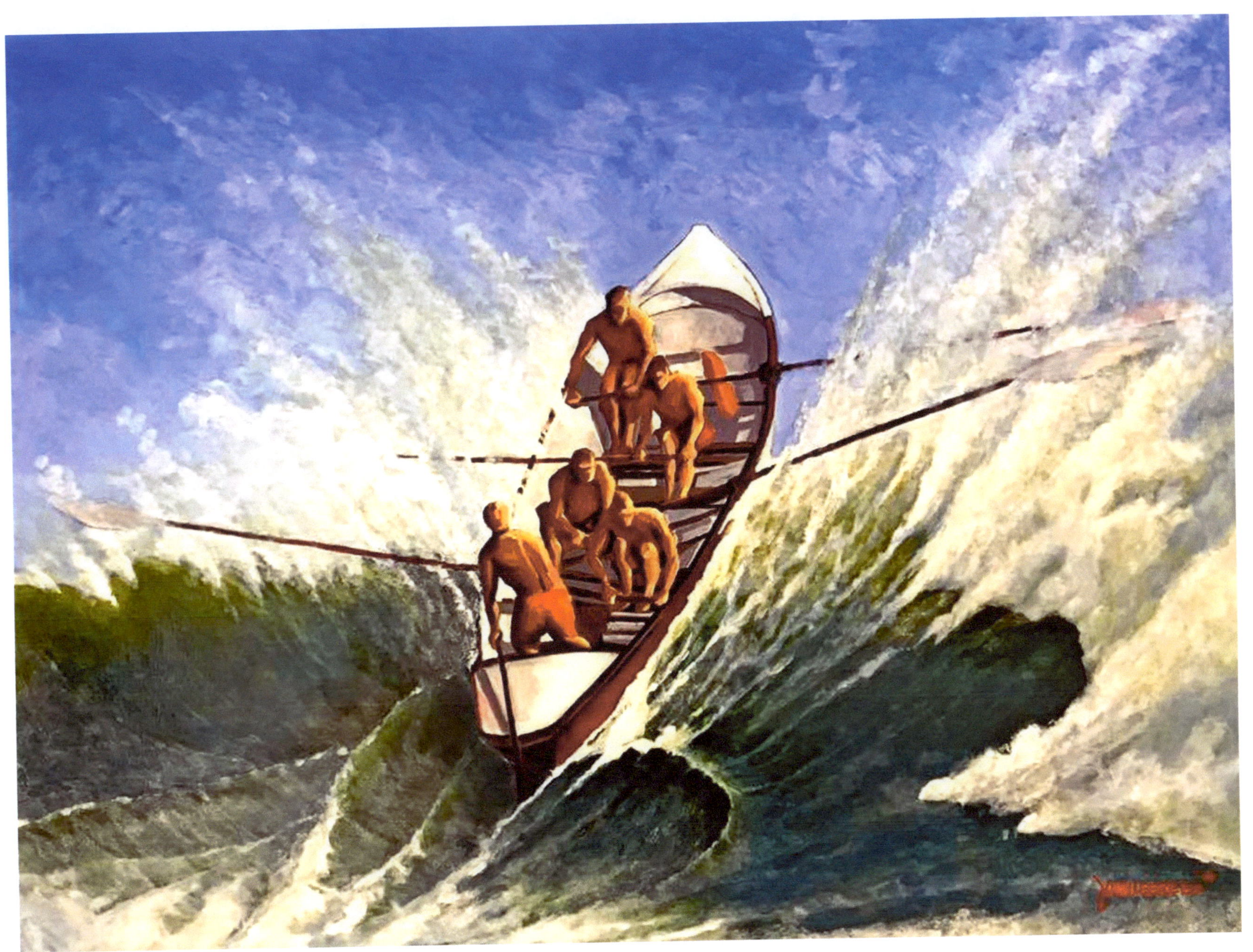

"Ocean Rescue" Oil on Canvas

During and after college, some of us even got to work on the beaches as lifeguards. This piece is a shout-out to the guard crews across the beaches of the planet: Real heroes that were doing it way before Baywatch was even a thing.

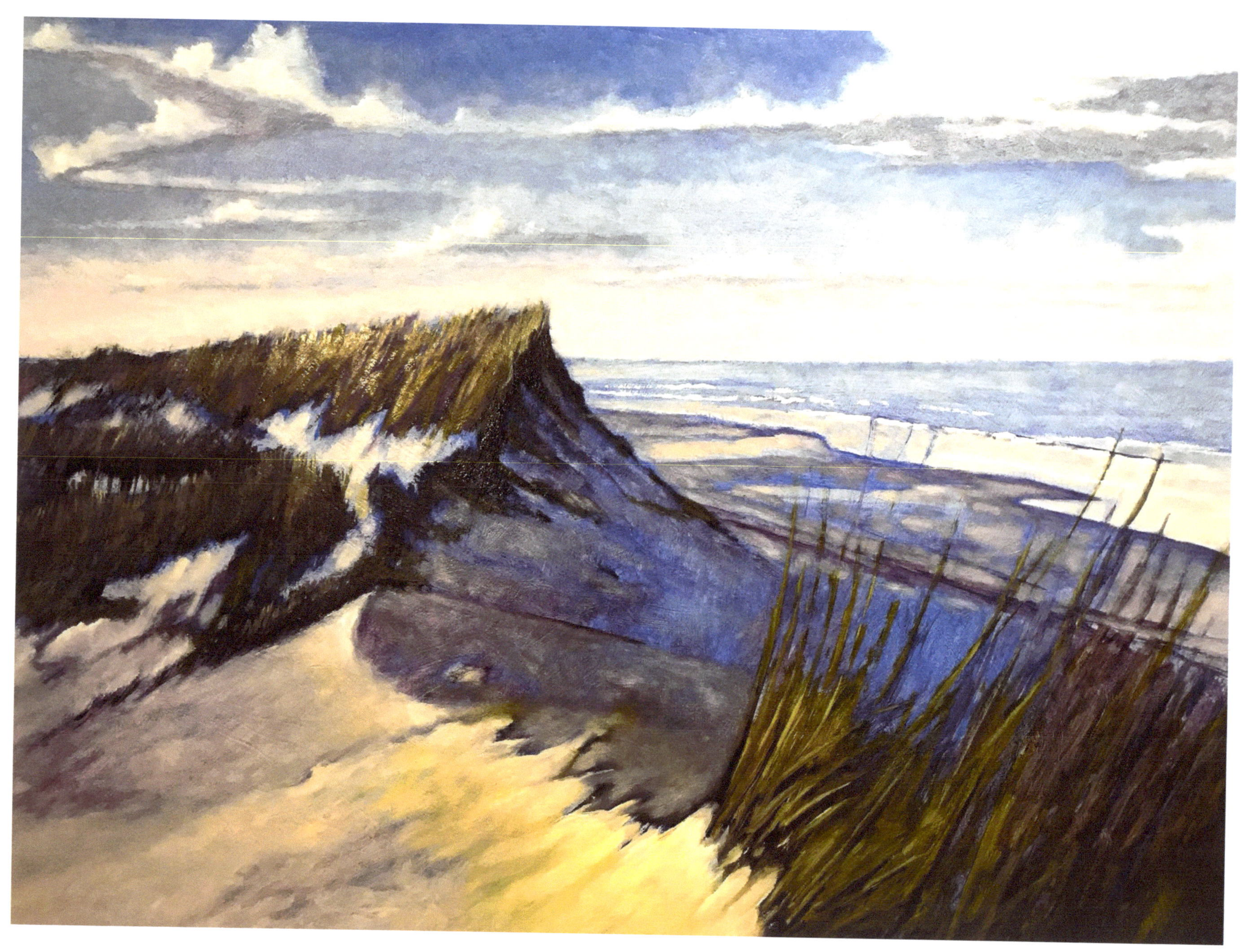

"Evening Dune" Oil on Canvas

The beaches of the East Coast provided everything we needed, and there was no better place to call home.

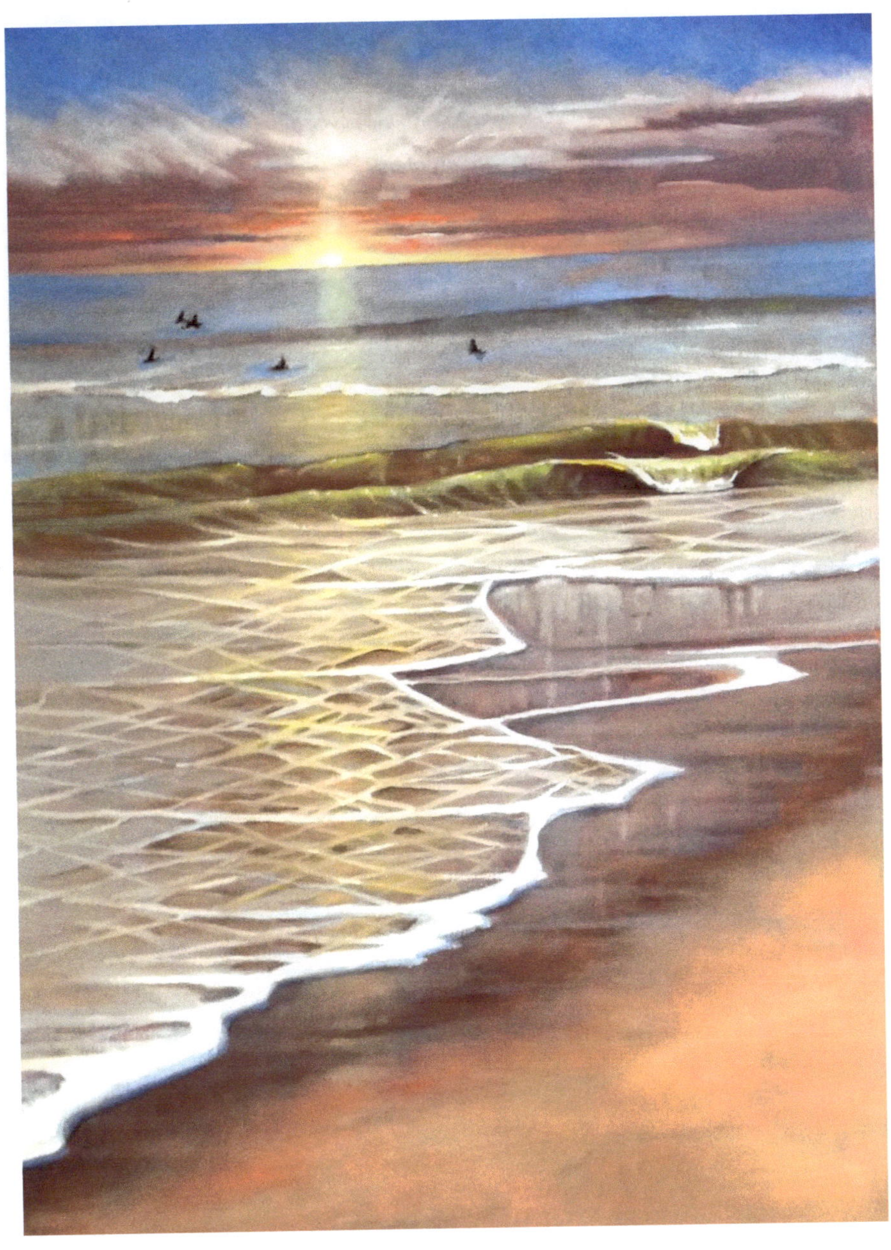

"Dawn Patrol at 77th" Oil on Canvas

Over the years, I've found nothing more satisfying than making art for people whom I love and respect. This was a commission for a dear friend who was missing her home on the North End of VB. Going into someone's home to see an original piece of my artwork on their wall, is like revisiting one of my children. There's nothing else like it!

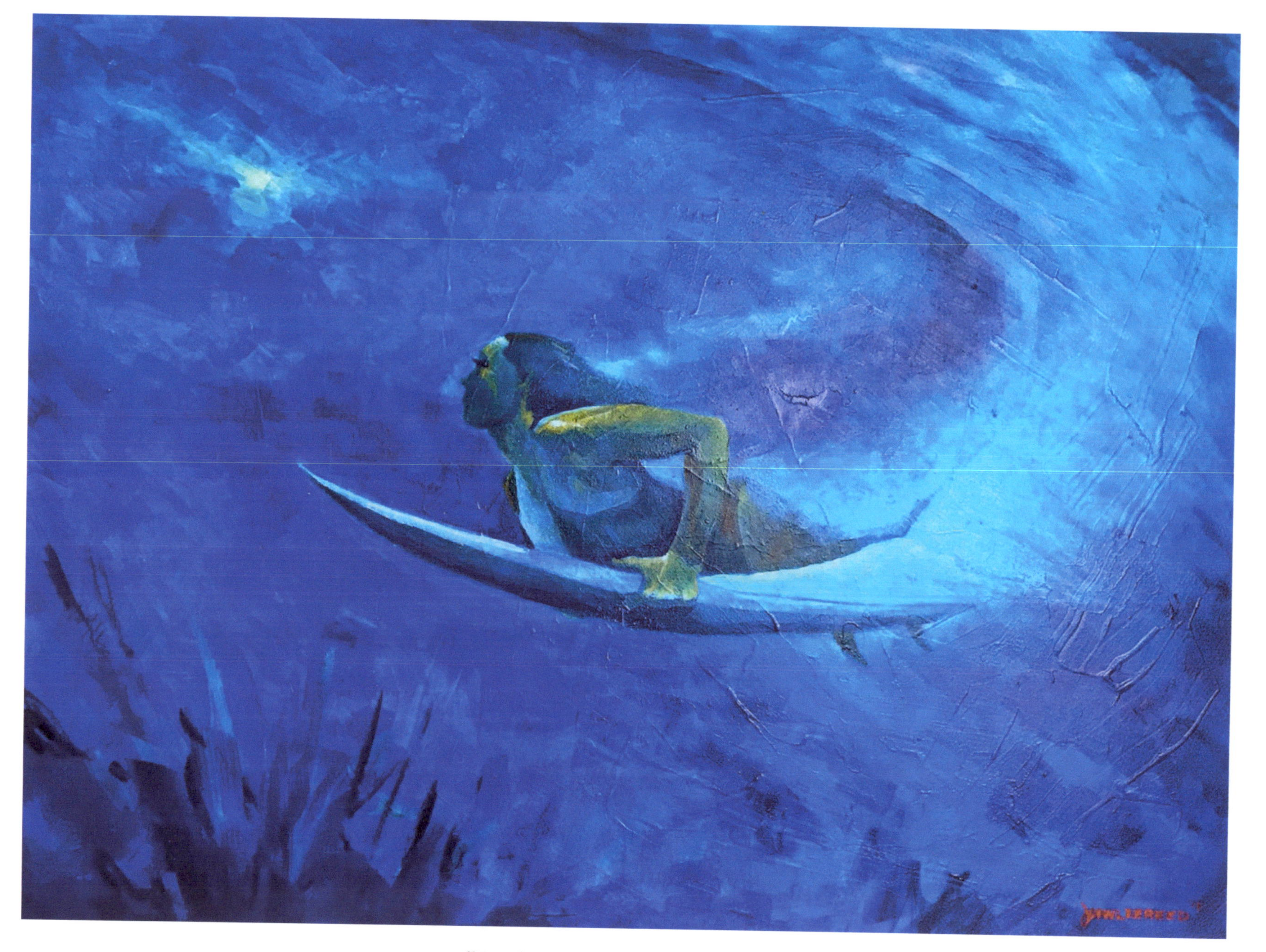

"Duck Dive" Acrylic on Canvas

Call me what you will, but I've always loved the subject of women's surfing. Women bring an elegance and grace to the sport that I love to try to capture on canvas.

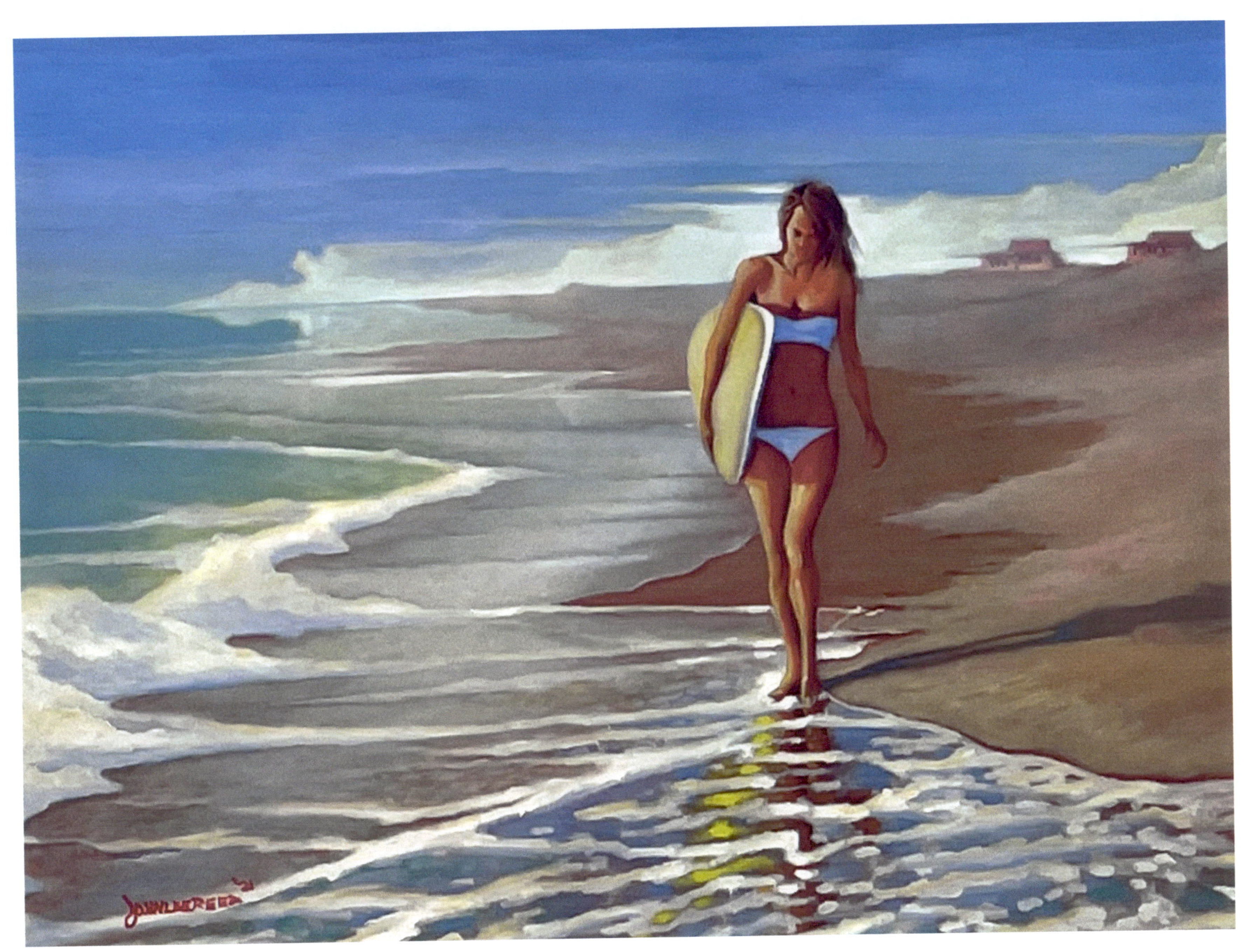

"Morning Workout" Oil on Canvas

Getting your surfing in before the afternoon breezes kickup is a routine that all East Coast surfers share, especially the beautiful ones.

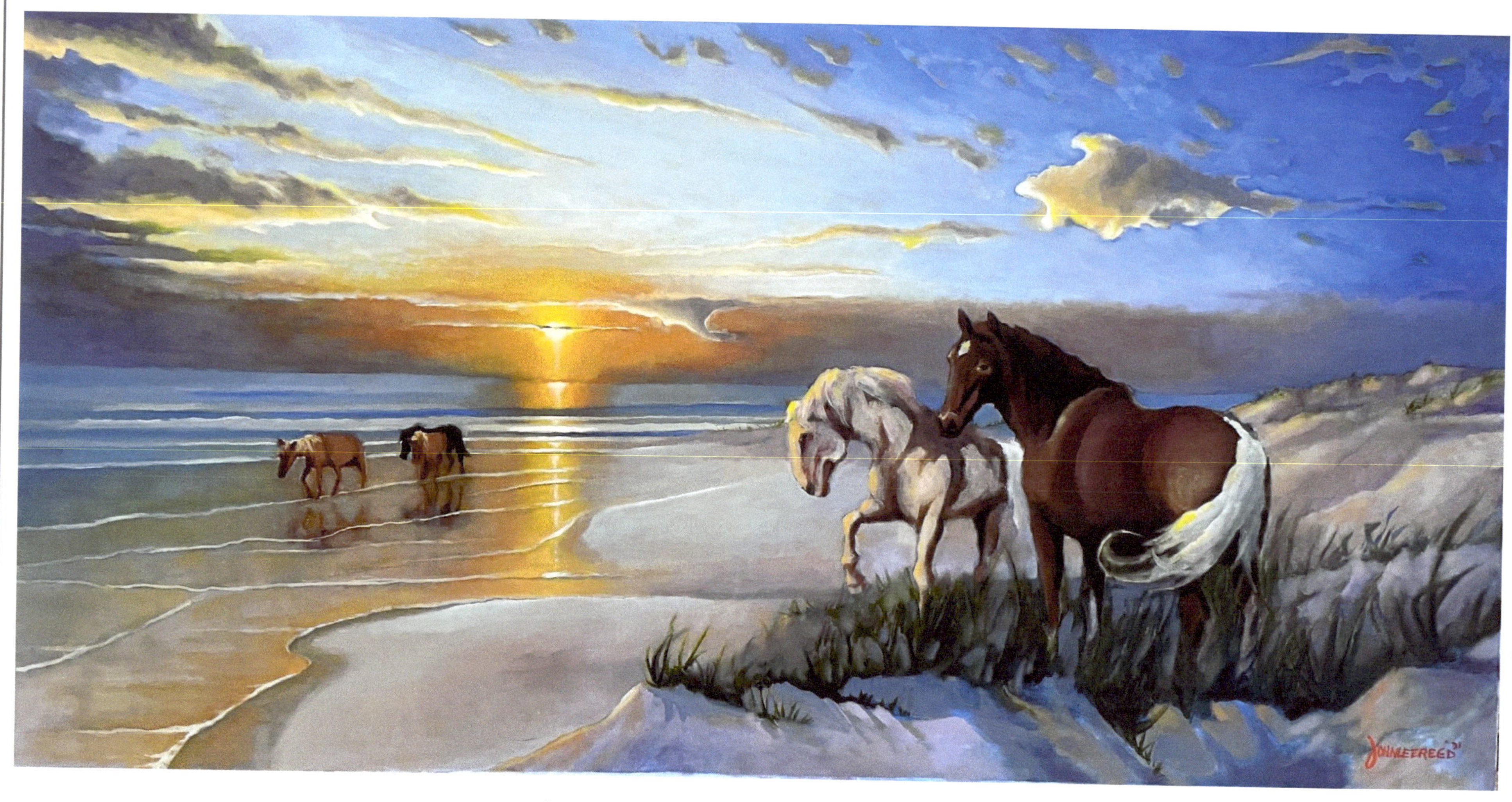

"The Local's Commute" Oil on Canvas

On the barrier islands outside of Virginia and North Carolina, there are still wild ponies that live their entire lives in freedom along the seashore. These beautiful creatures revive my hope for reincarnation.

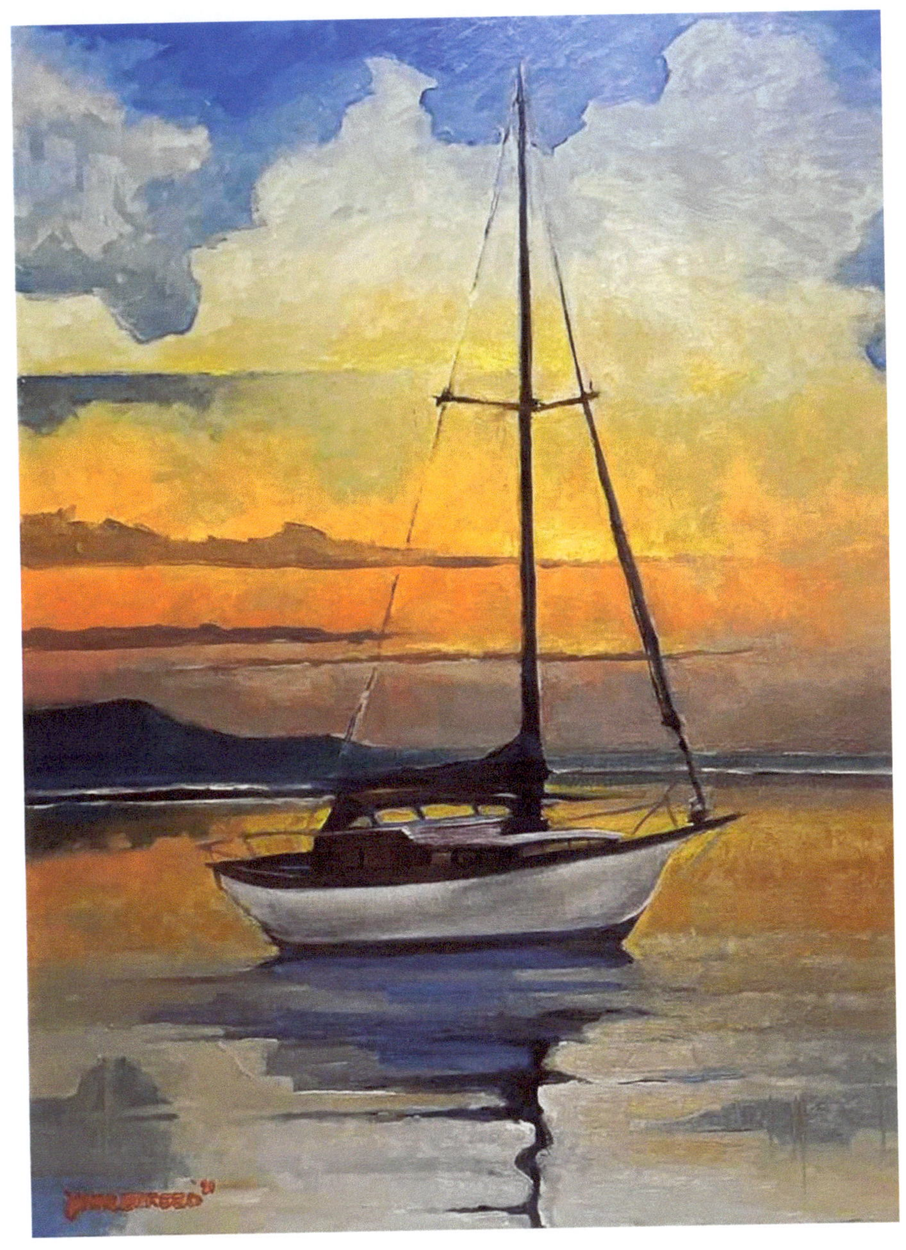

"Sunset Harbor" Oil on Canvas

Day yields to night and it's easy to get lost in how you can be better tomorrow. However, the fleeting beauty of the tropical island sunset is there to remind you that you really own nothing but the moment, and it's there that you should reside.

Lessons from Heaven

The great John Wooden said that everyone deals with failure - that's a part of life. When you fail, however, make sure to "Fail Forward." Looking back, many a Guardian Angel had bailed my young, dumb ass out of tight situations I had gotten into one way or the other. The first one that I ever recognized, however, was an 87-year-old Catholic nun named Sister Agatha.

It was 1988, and I was trying to get to sleep in a cold and unfamiliar hospital bed at Virginia Beach General Hospital. I was alone in my room late on the night before the doctors were going to cut me open and extract my right testicle early the next morning. The only way they could determine what kind of cancer I had was to remove the little dude and put him under a microscope to see whether I was going to live or die.

At 28, it was my first introduction to mortality.

I was lying there alone, completely petrified and totally broken, when the large door to my room slowly opened, and

The Angel stepped in.

Just as Christ arrived in Bethlehem as an underwhelming figure seated on the back of a lowly donkey, in walked Sister Agatha, silently flowing like the turning of a midnight ocean tide. She was no more than 4 feet tall, wrinkled and spectacled, wearing the simple black robes of the Catholic Diocese. I would love to tell you all that she was glowing, but that would be a total exaggeration.

The Angel approached my bed and introduced herself to me as I made every effort to sit up and acknowledge her. We talked for a moment, and I understood that she was totally appraised of my situation. With the necessary introductions out of the way, I simply asked her:

"Sister, what do you think God has in store for me tomorrow?" With that came a smile on her face that I will always remember.

"God," she said, "has a plan." "He often works in ways that most people have a hard time recognizing. He has a plan for you. He just doesn't want you to screw it up." The words hit me like an unexpected, rogue wave. That simple sentence changed my perspective from:

"Why is this happening to me?" to "How can I do a better job of living my life in harmony with The Universe?"

I had flamed out on Madison Avenue, failed to make my mark as a Sporting Goods salesman, and only reached "Average White Boy" status as an athlete. I began to examine the true gifts that had been given me, and all navigational beacons pointed to my art. It was time to "fail forward."

The Angel disappeared into the quiet hallways of the hospital before I even had a chance to say, "Thank you."

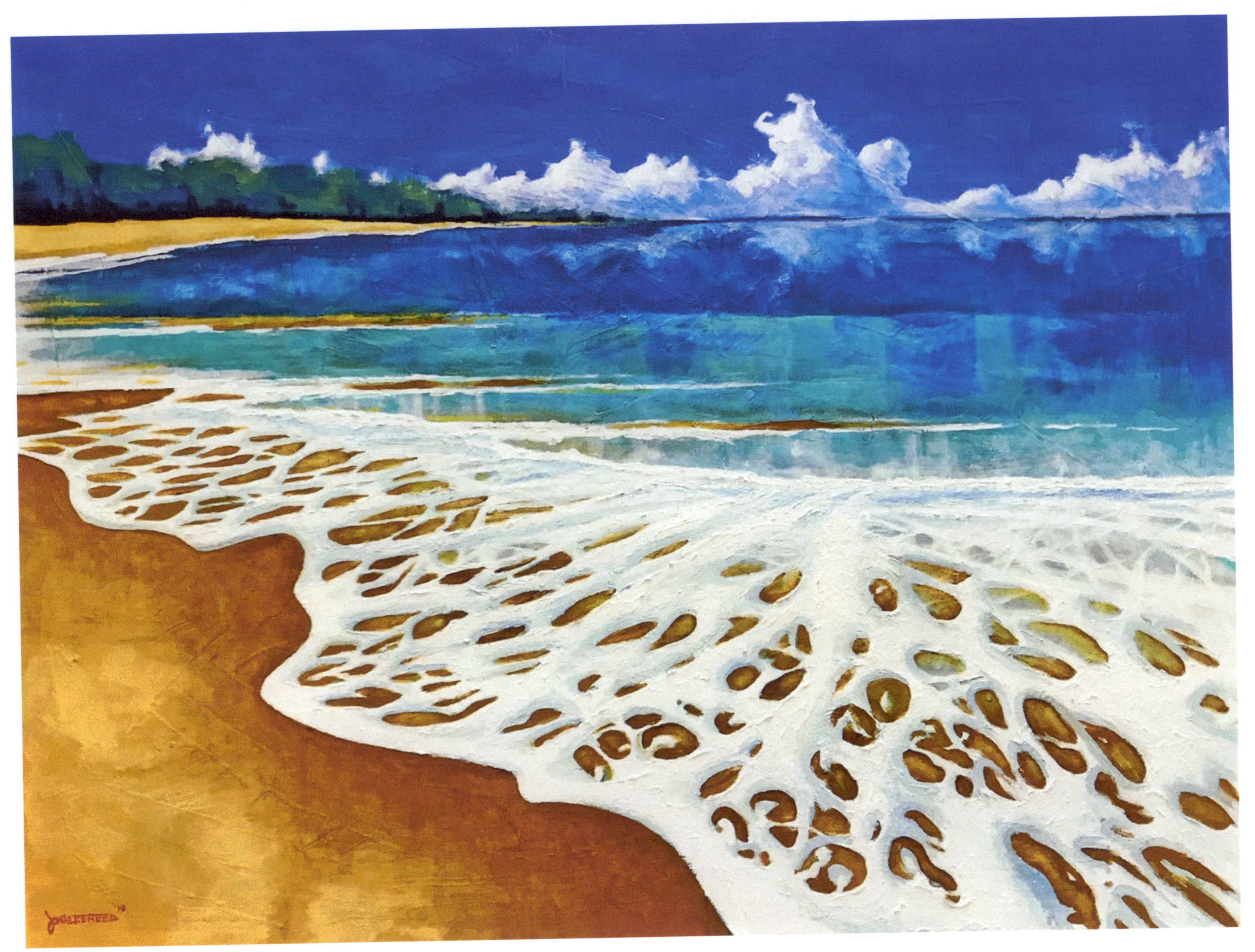

"After the Storm" Oil on Canvas

With the storm gently fading over the horizon, a better understanding of my new direction and brighter days ahead, I escaped to Florida to start a new career as the artist that I always knew I could be.

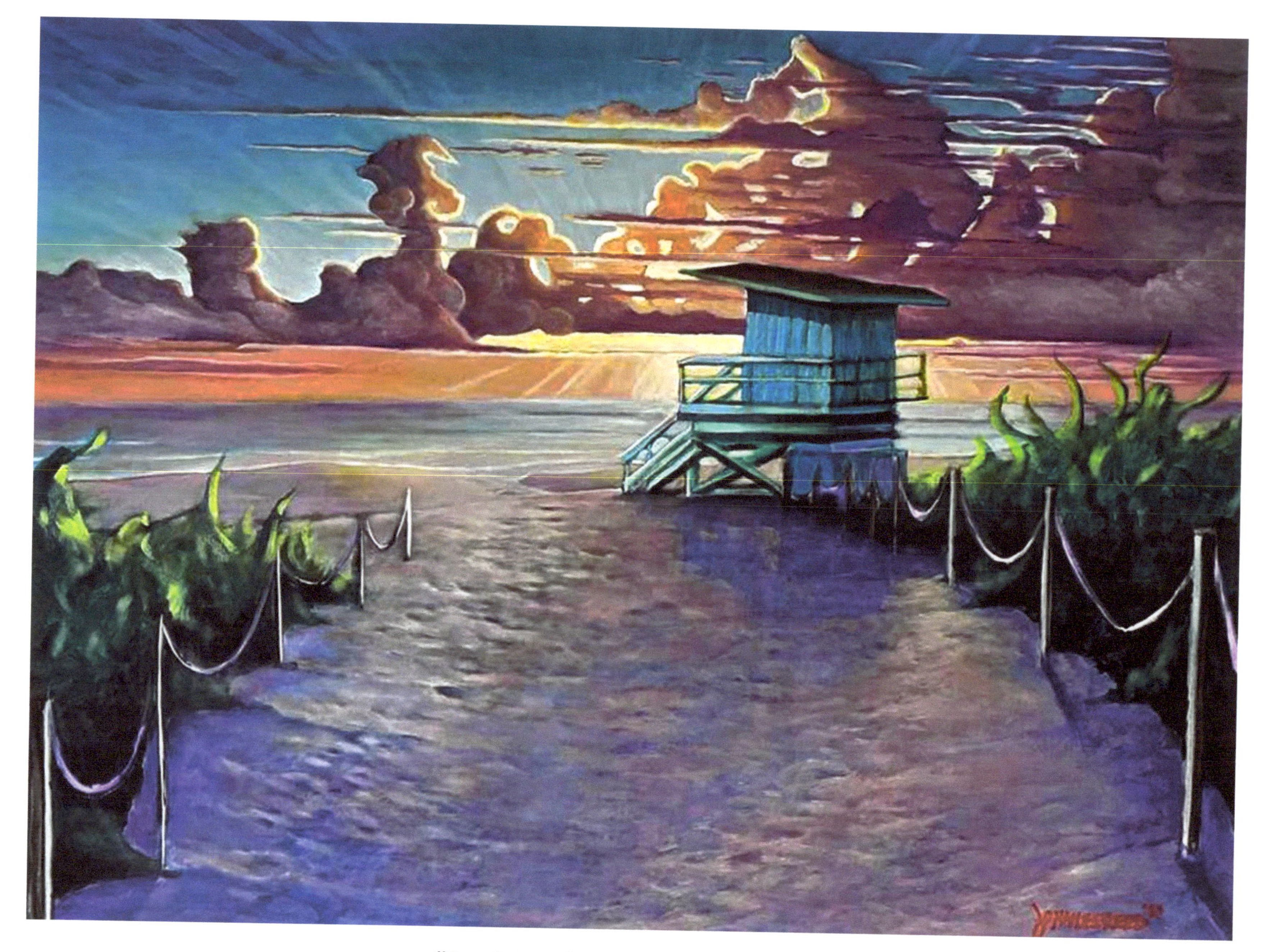

"South Beach Sunrise" Oil on Canvas

South Florida always seemed like Mecca to me. I arrived in a beat-up old Datsun B210 with questionable breaks and $4. in my pocket. It was the happiest I'd been in my entire life. Luckily, I had friends there who helped me along the way.

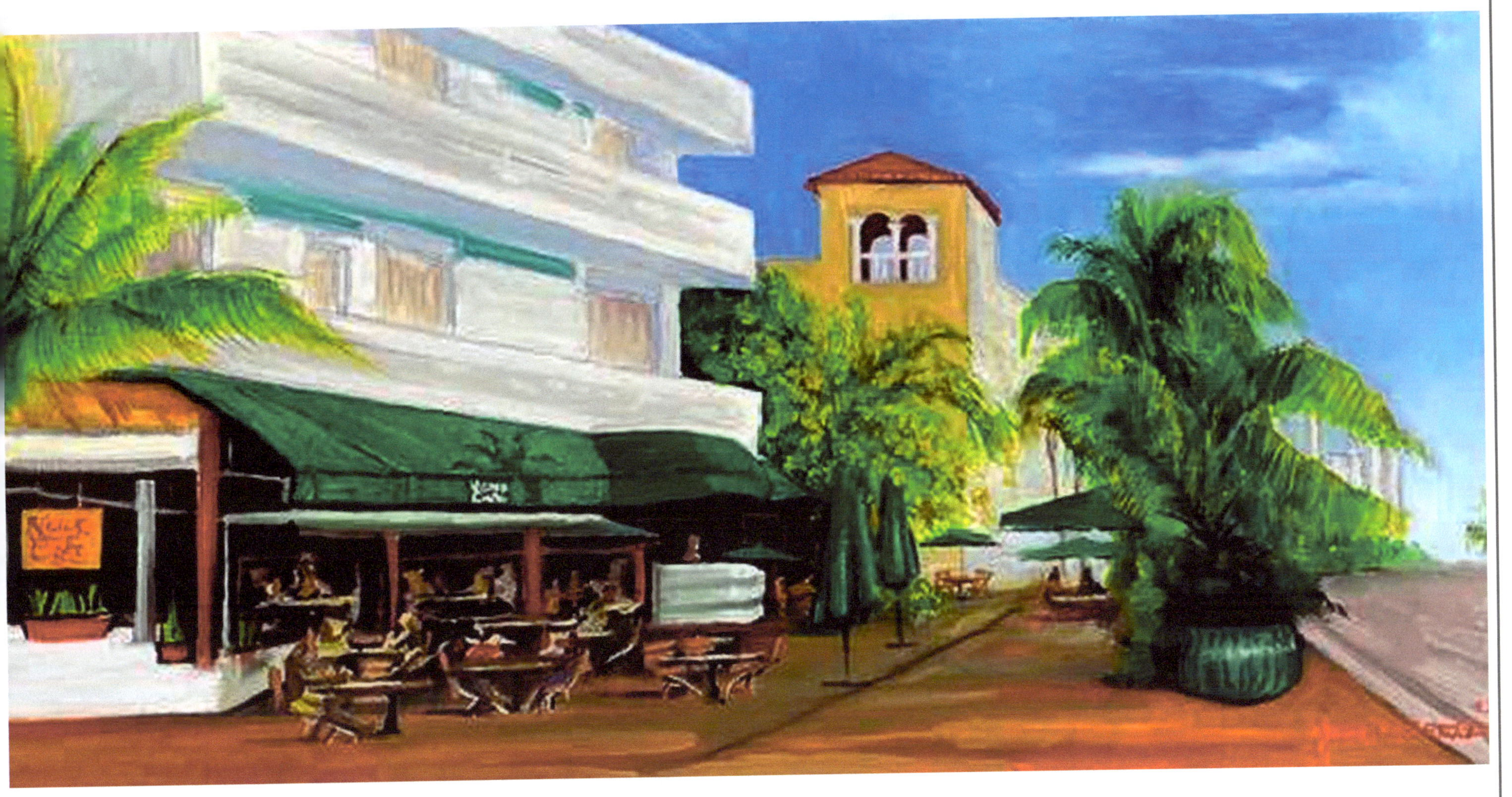

"The News" Oil on Canvas

South Miami Beach in the early to mid '90s was just catching fire. The transformation from sleepy retirement community to Worldwide Hip Hop, Destination Resort was only beginning. In those days, there were still vacancies for underpaid artists and an assortment of other colorful characters including sailors, seasonal super models and vagabond creatives of all types. I had a job working with some of the most talented artists in the country designing T-shirts and Beach Towels for Disney, Warner Bros., and many other first tier entertainment companies. I rented a sweet, little apartment 2 blocks from Ocean Drive and the News Café was one of my favorite hang outs. I was still as penny-less as a pauper, but I had a refrigerator full of cold cervezas and friends from all over the country flying in to sleep on my couch every weekend!

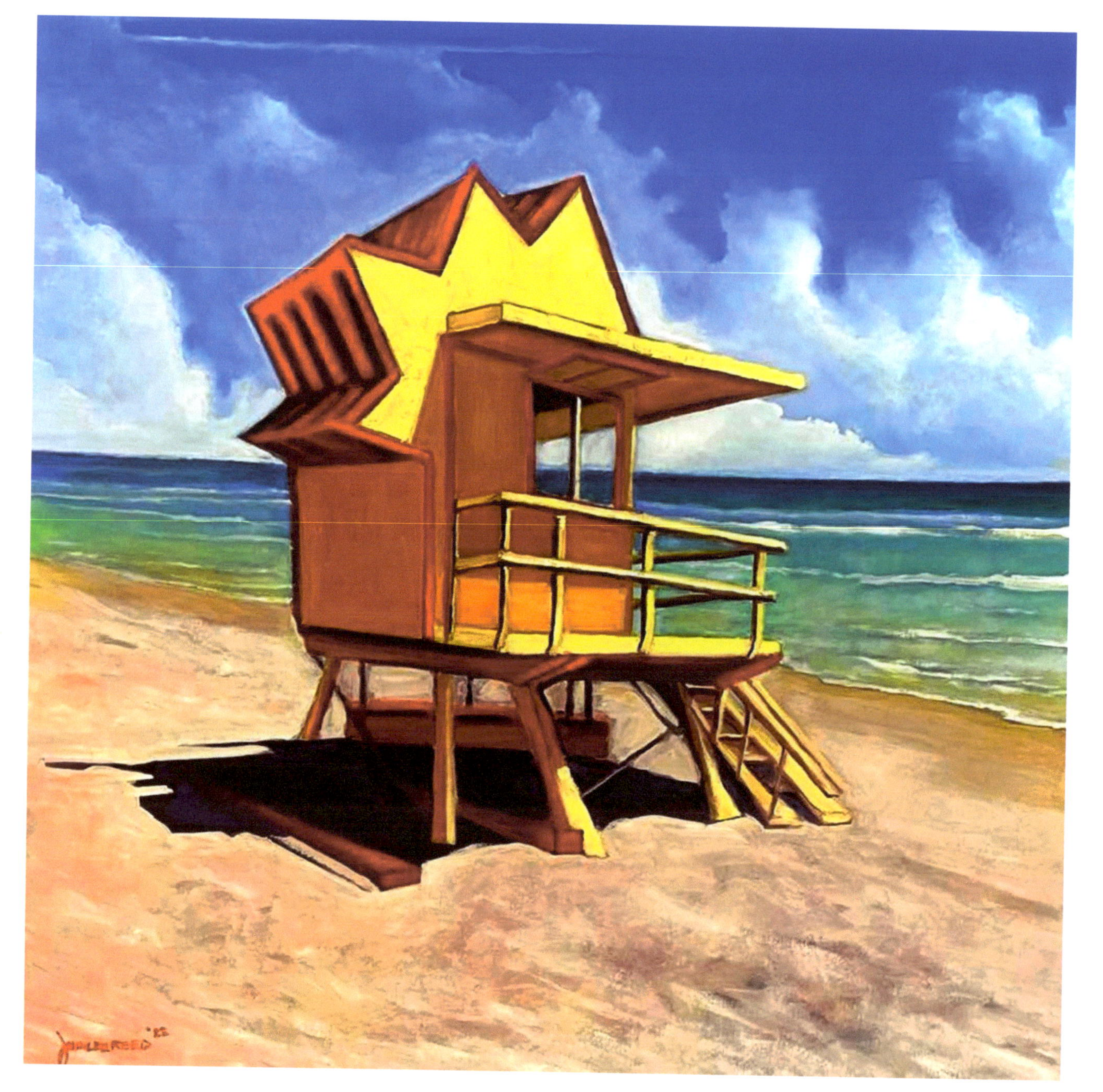

"The Lisa Simpson" Oil on Canvas

Miami Beach and its Art Deco Influence inspired me as it spilled out from the hotels all the way to the water's edge.

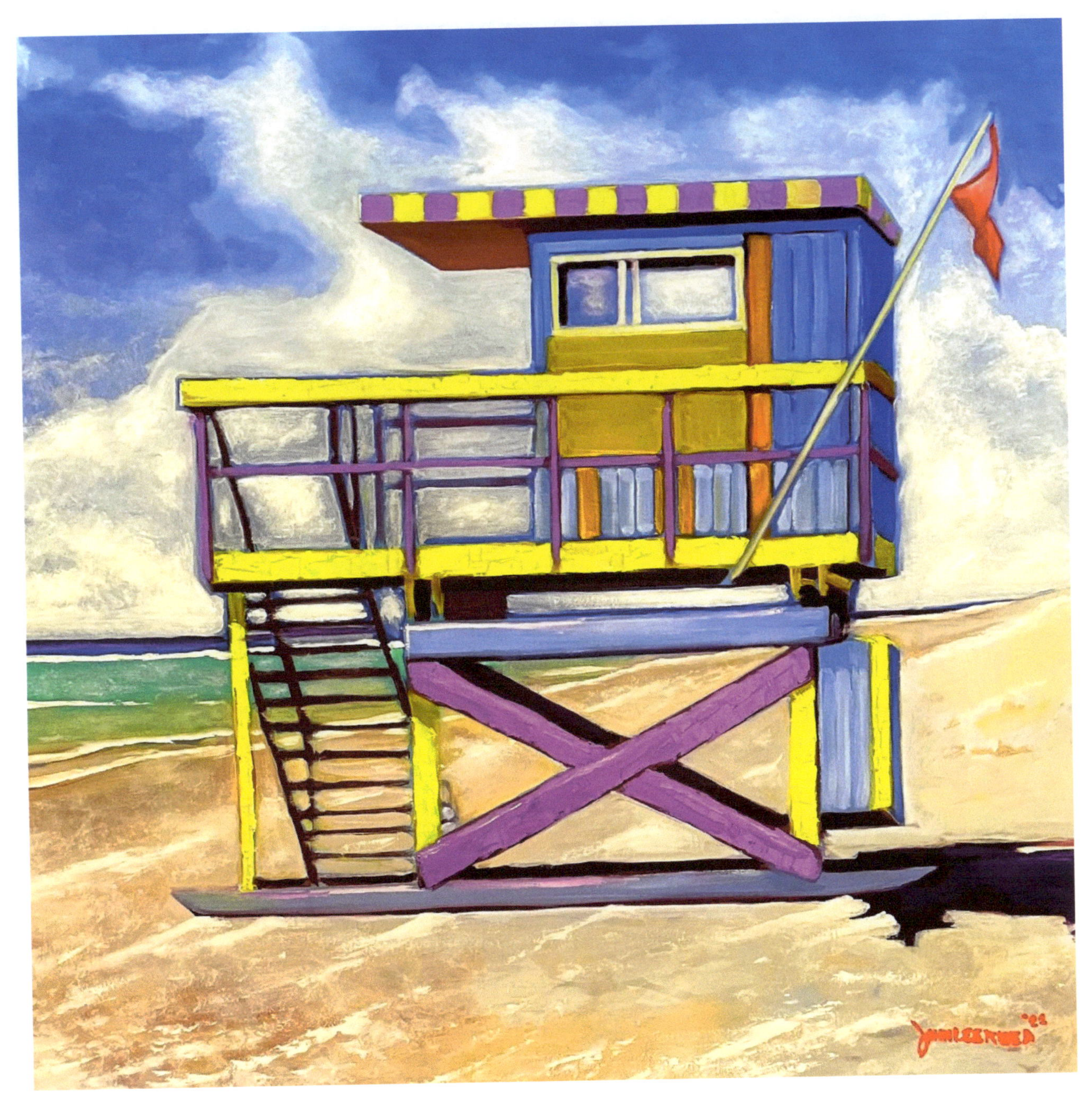

"Guard House Glamour" Oil on Canvas

SoBe had it all: The art, the beach, the sunshine and the exotic and colorful presence of an international creative influence.

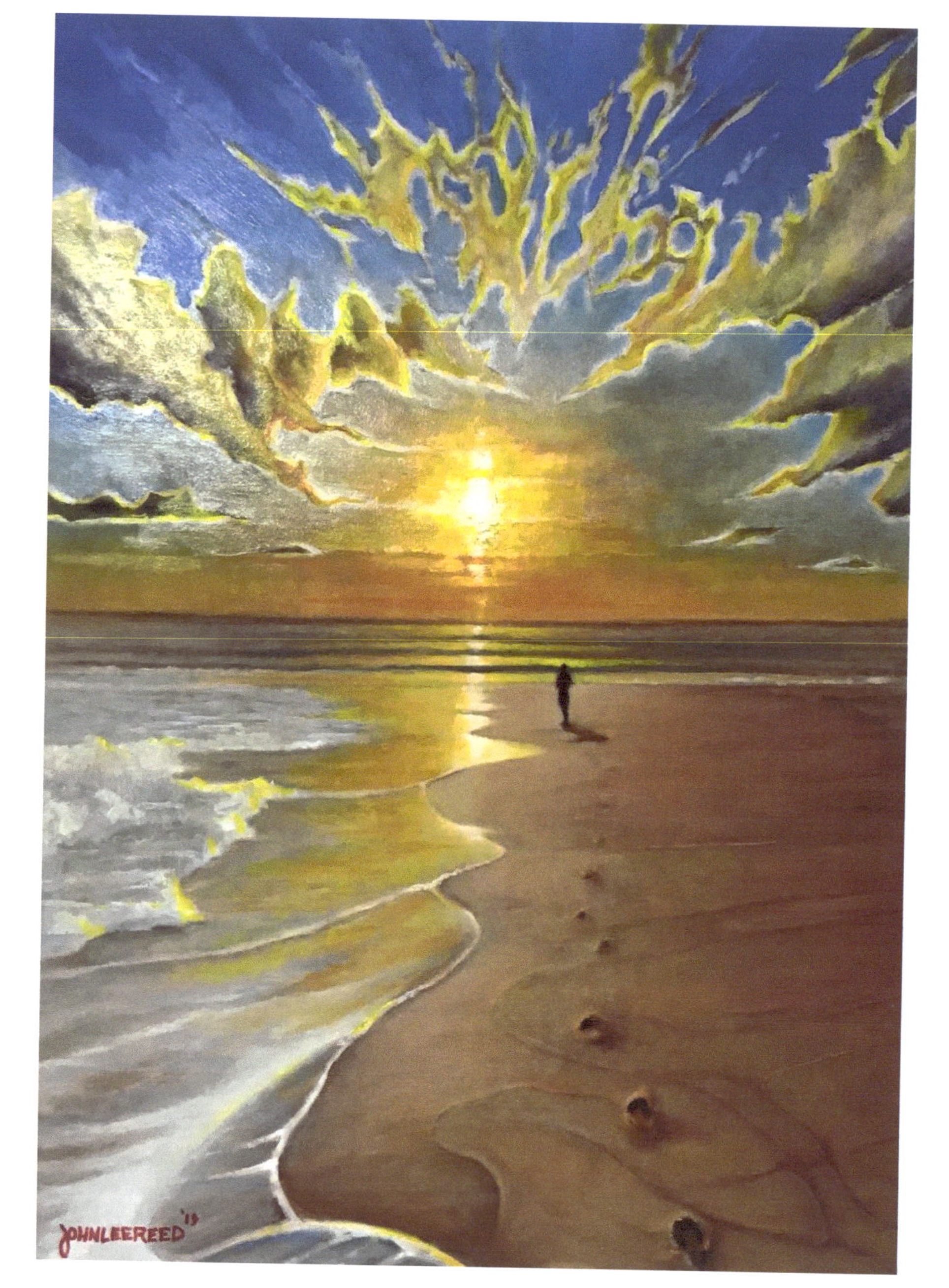

"Rum Cay" Oil on Canvas

Even more exciting was the idea that there were tropical paradises just waiting for me to explore.

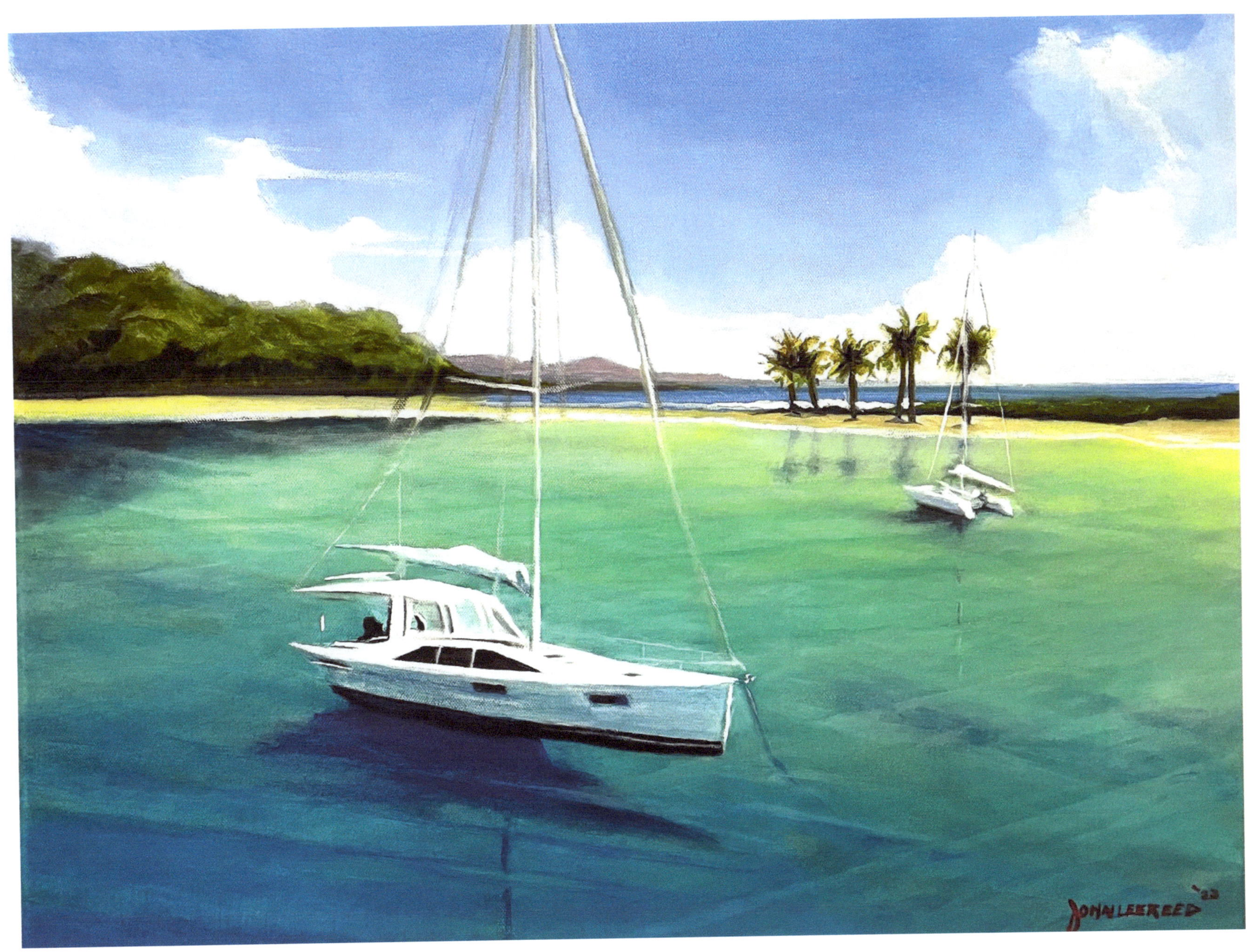

"Caribbean Layover" Oil on Canvas

Living and working as an artist in South Florida led me to discover my love for sailing. With the Bahamas and the Caribbean in reach, I began to discover a part of the world that would call to me for the rest of my life.

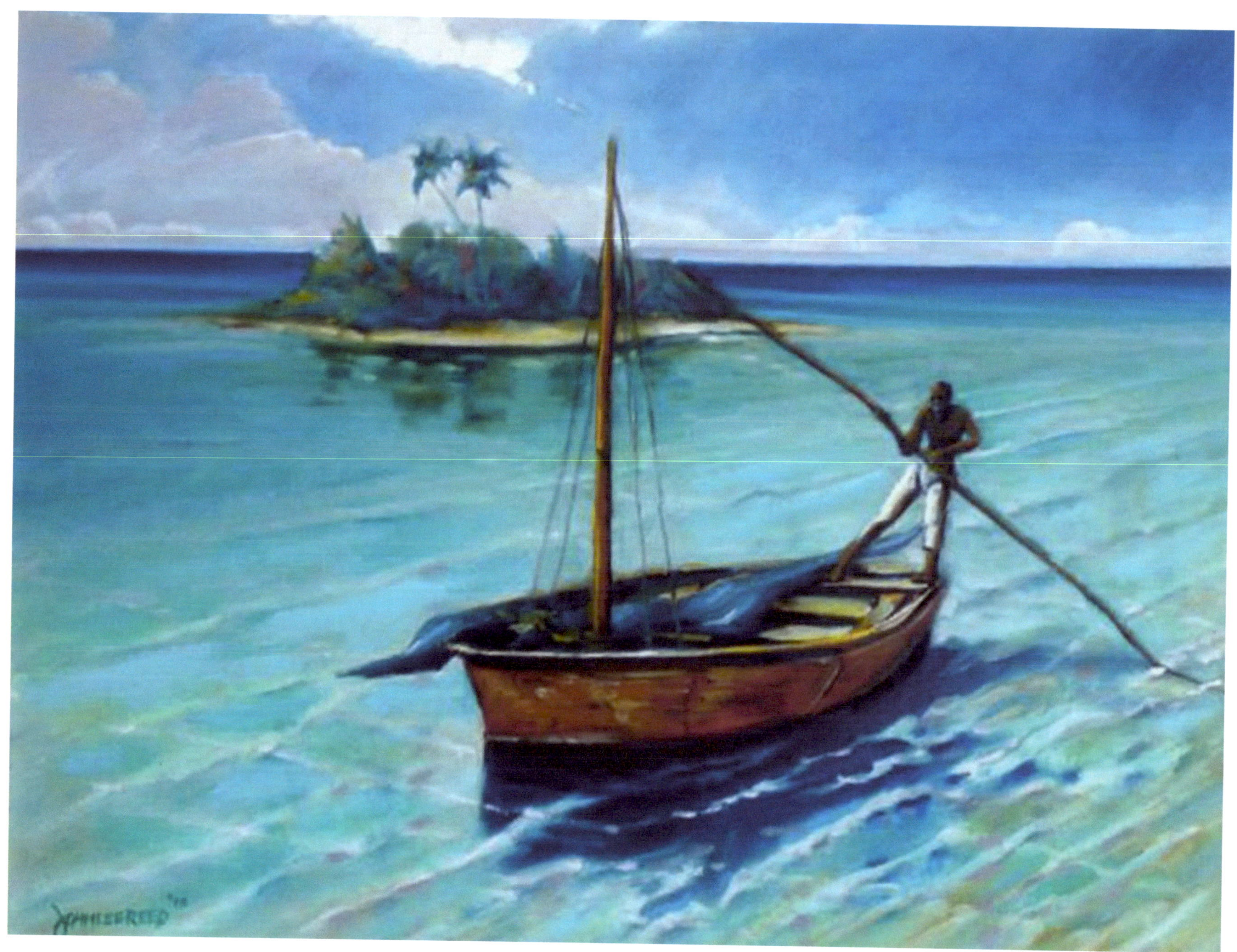

"Polling In" Oil on Canvas

Island life became one of my favorite creative subjects and the colors of the Caribbean dominated my palette.

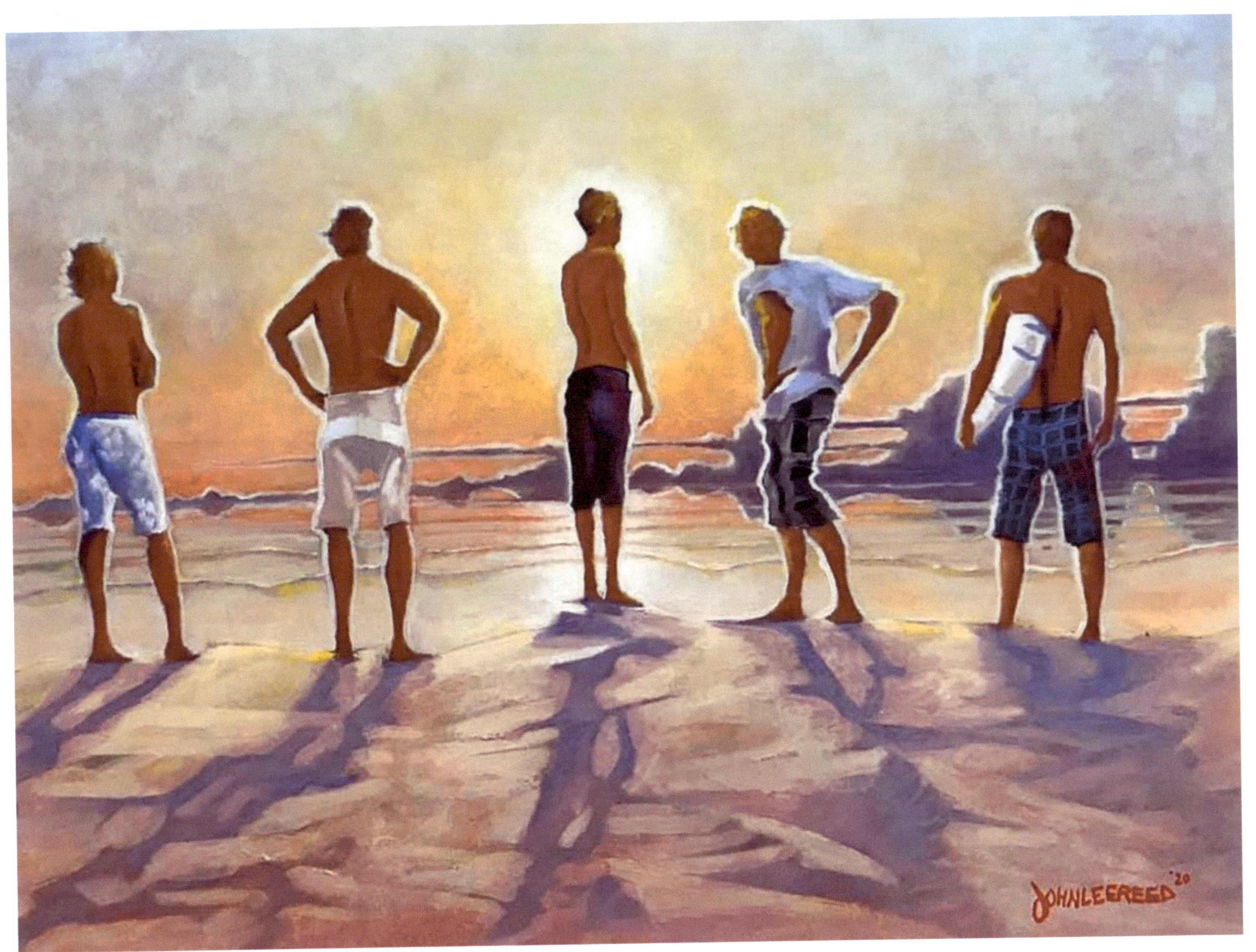

"Waitin' on Waves" Oil on Canvas

Still, as surfers on the East Coast, we spent a lot of time watching the weather forecasts and waiting to get the opportunity to do some real surfing.

Flowing into Respectability

South Florida was an amazing and enlightening experience for me as an artist and a person.

I was enjoying myself immensely.

The vibrant and colorful culture was so excitingly different from the world I knew growing up in Virginia. For the first time in my life, I loved going to work every day. I couldn't afford a car, so I either had to bum a ride or get up very early and ride the bus into Hialeah for work each day.

Many a morning, I would get up before the heat of the sun and walk out to the bus stop on Washington Avenue, two blocks from the beach. The smells of the streets, combined with the fresh, salty air, made it a different adventure with every single sunrise. With my sketch pad in hand, I would often grab a Café Cubano from the early food truck and wait patiently for the number 3 bus into Miami. Those early morning bus rides were loaded with local farmers and craftsmen taking their goods into the city for sale or trade. I often sat quietly sketching next to neighboring entrepreneurs taking their crafted items, boxes of fresh tamales, or caged roosters into market. After only a couple of months, I became a bit of a number 3 bus celebrity, as I often ripped out and gave my pencil sketches to the subjects of my morning portraiture exercise. I only spoke a minimal amount of Spanish, but I was communicating just fine in my new environment.

I was just another working-class Floridian schlepping my butt through the heat into work,

but I loved every minute of it!

The only problem was that I was into my mid-30s, and I was making only enough money to get through the week. After a couple of years as a lead designer, I knew I needed to take the next step and direct an art department of my own.

That opportunity came along 1500 miles to the west, in a place I had only read about. I packed up my surf trunks and traded in my surfboard for a mountain bike and a snowboard.

I was off to make my mark in Denver, Colorado.

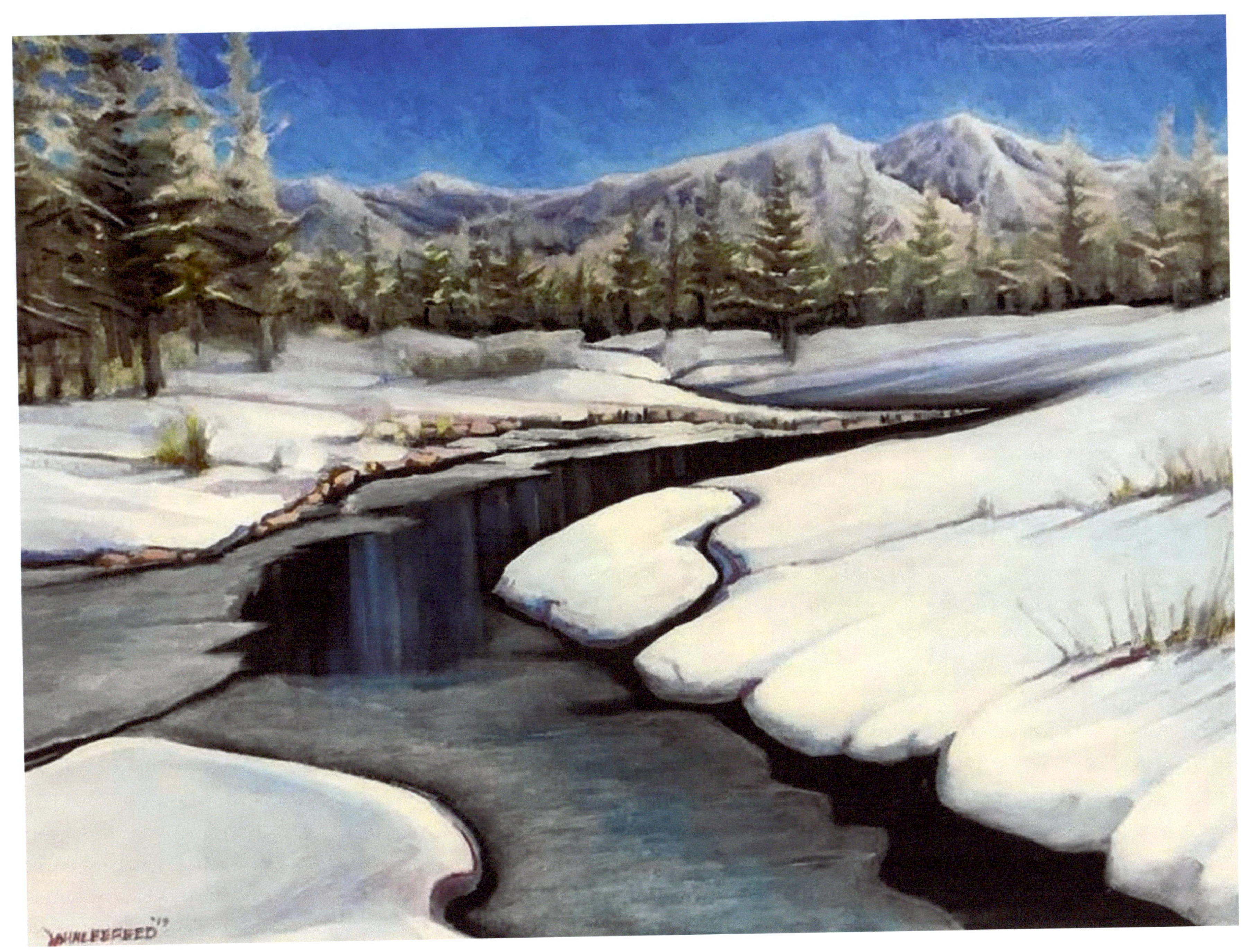

"Creek to Breck" Oil on Birch Panel

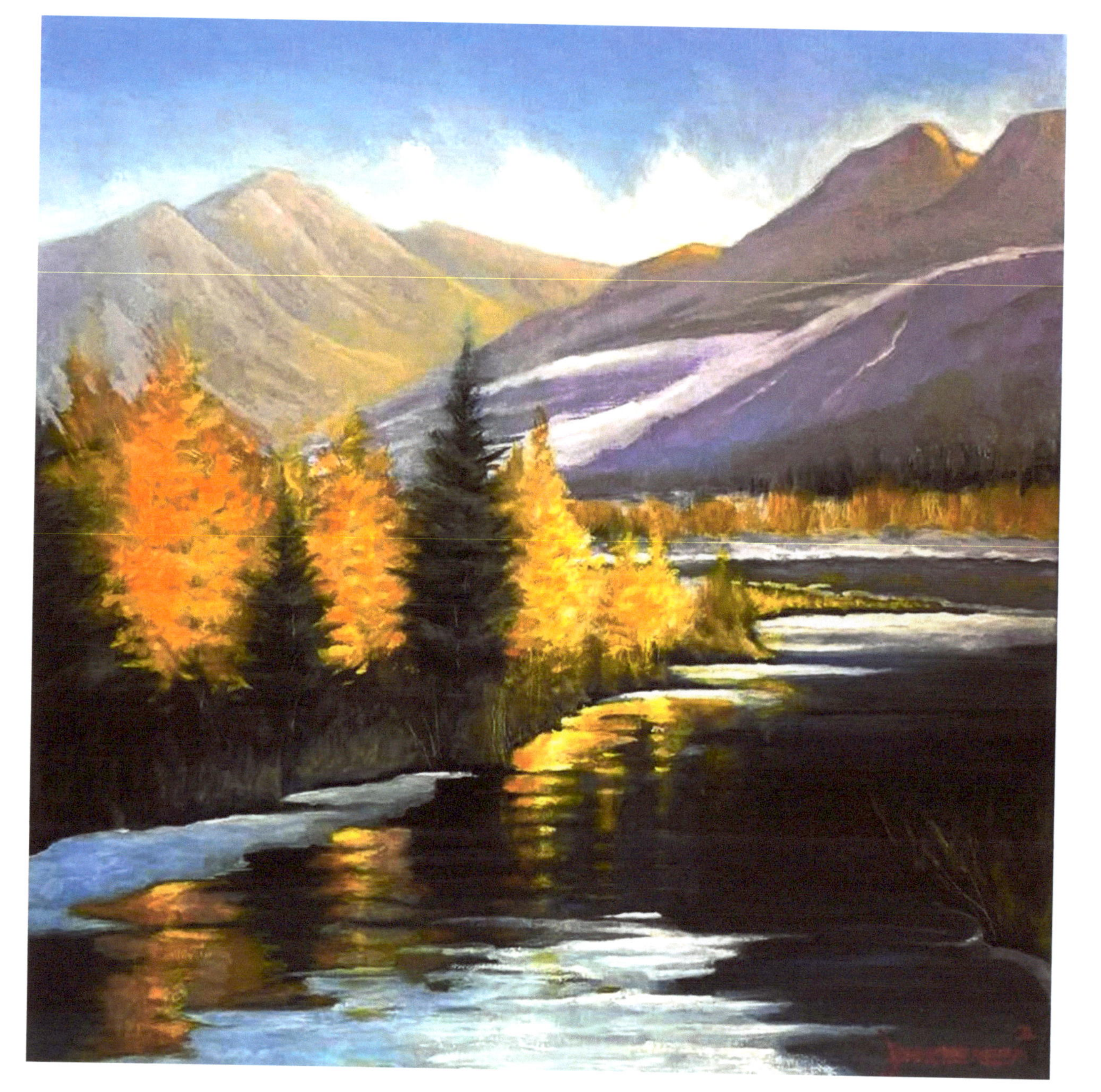

"High Country Transitions" Oil on Canvas

The Rocky Mountains were full of artistic inspiration for me. As the fall arrives in the high country the colors blaze with magnificence.

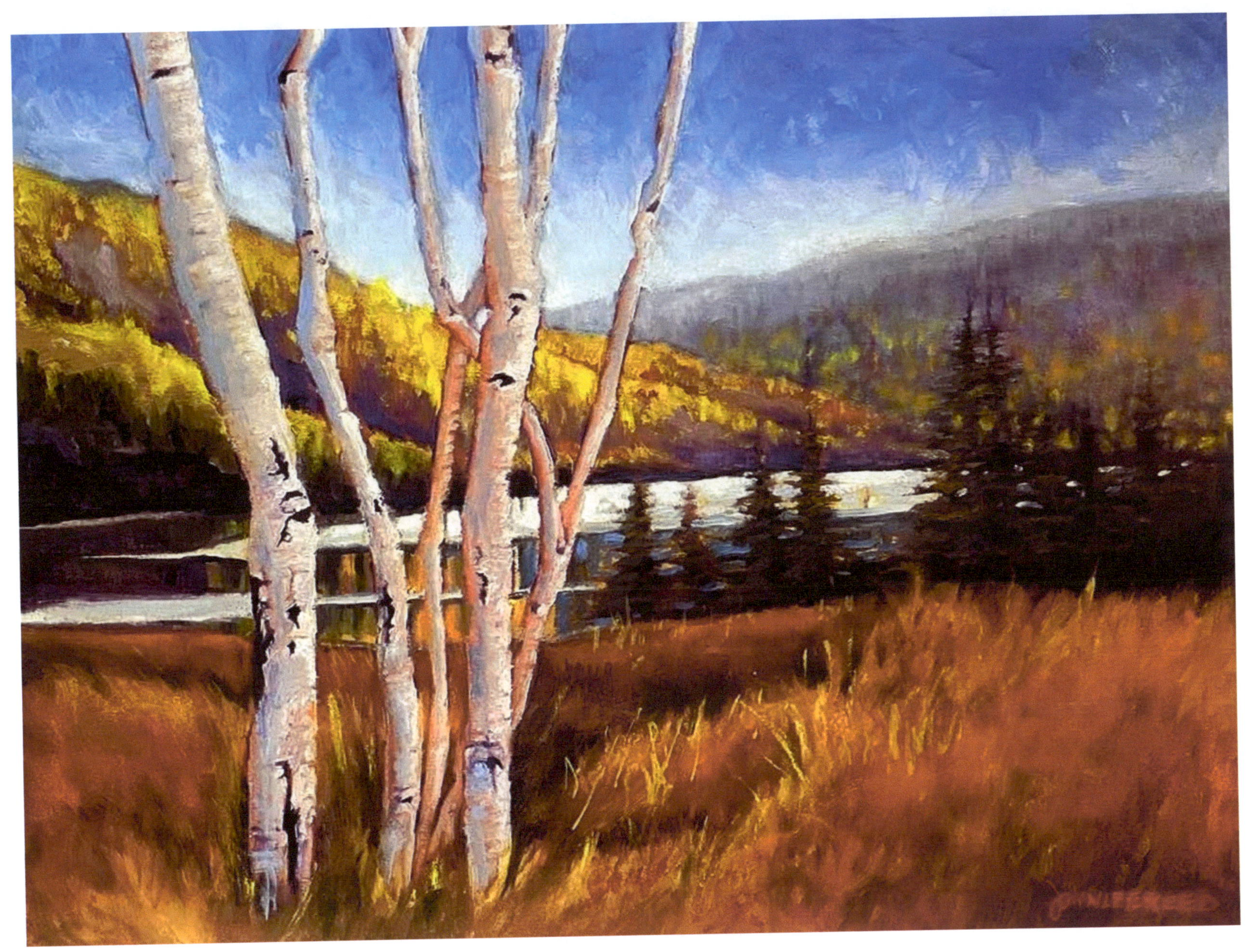

"Aspen Grove" Oil on Canvas

I missed the glory of the changing seasons while living in the tropics. I found 'Secret Spots" in the foothills and the valleys of the Rocky Mountains that rivaled those of my favorite beaches. Living in (not just visiting) different parts of the country helped to broaden my perspective.

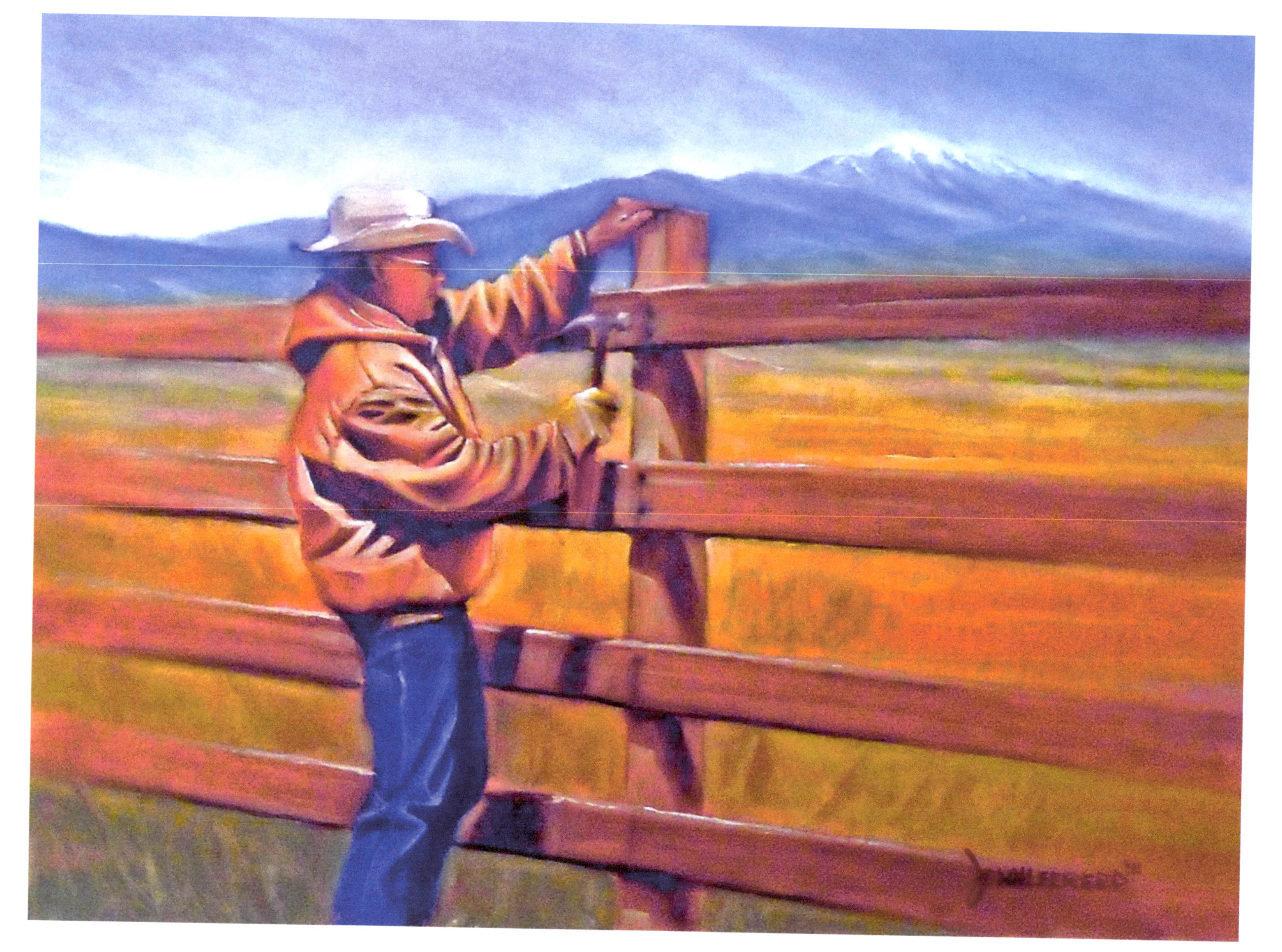

"On the Fence" Oil on Canvas

I was a little concerned that I might be "a fish outta water" in my new digs. That concern went away when I soon began some serious snowboarding in the winter and mountain biking in the summer. I fell in love with the hard-working people and their outdoor lifestyle. In many respects, Colorado saved me by broadening my perspective. Little did I know that She would have an even bigger impact on my life moving forward.

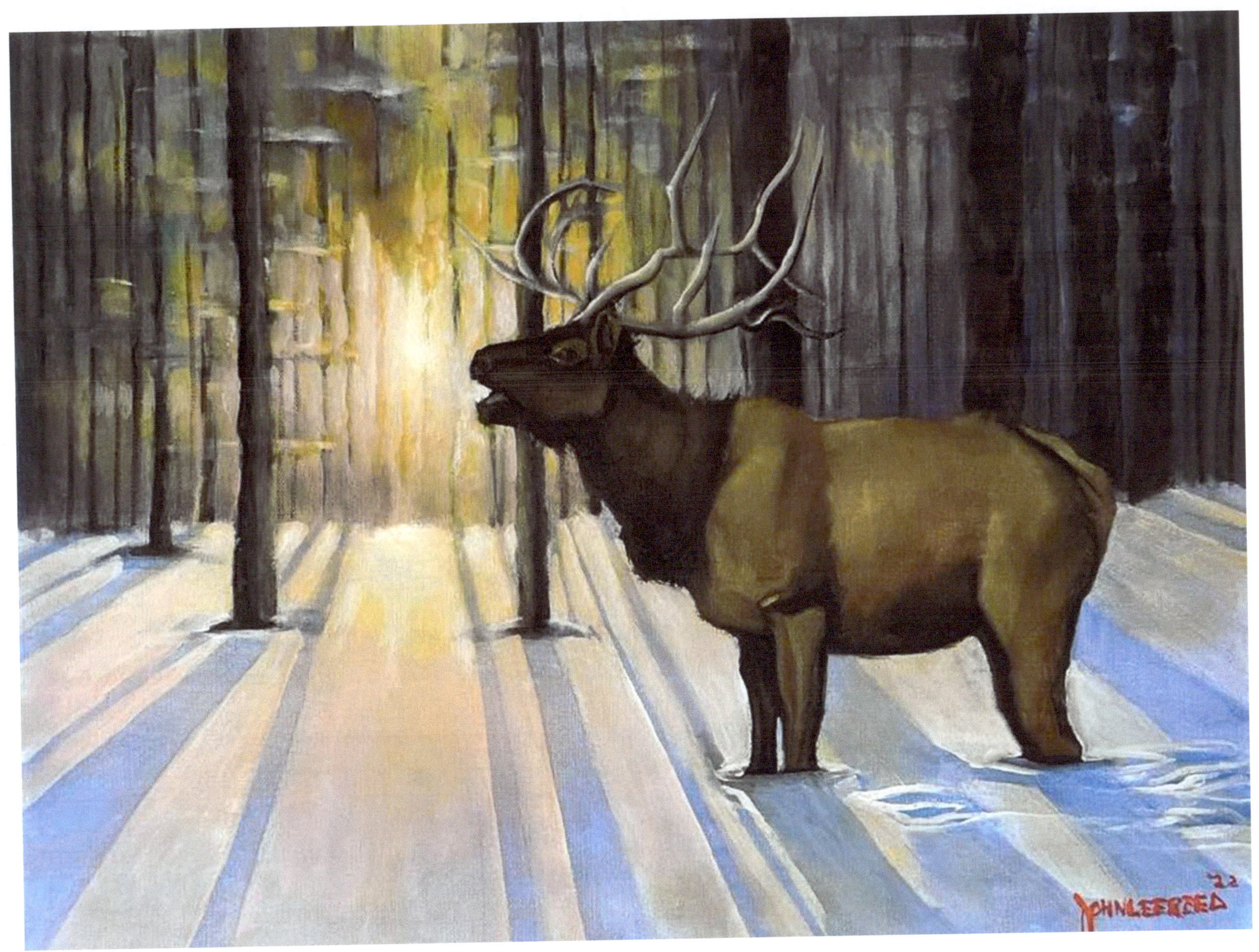

"Morning Roll Call" Oil on Canvas

The Bull Elk is making his morning bugle calls. I was out on my own, making a living doing what I loved, but there was still something missing. Like this big fella, I was searching for just a little bit more in life.

The Vibration of The Universe

After a successful several years building and running an Art department for a 50-state souvenir company in Denver, there was still something missing in my life. I had built a dynamic, technologically updated art department and traveled the world sourcing products in Europe, Japan, China, Korea, and Taiwan. My art was all over the country, albeit on coffee mugs, t-shirts, and shot glasses. I was proving to everyone, most importantly myself, that I could actually carve out a decent living creating art. Yet, there was still a void that I knew I had to address.

I believe in Vibration.

If you want The Universe to provide an opportunity for you, you need to vocalize it. The vibration of our speech has powers that we are only beginning to understand. In my opinion, prayer should not be silent, but it does need to be focused and consistent.

I yearned to find the right partner and start a family.

From my 13th-story apartment balcony, overlooking the golden dome of the state capitol building of Colorado and the front range of the Rocky Mountains, I voiced my request.

Every day.

Maybe it was simply an exercise that focused my thought patterns on a single objective. Maybe it was the adage that if you define and create a void, The Universe will work to fill it.

Either way, after consistently asking The Universe for what I wanted, my wishes were granted in ways far beyond my wildest imagination. I soon found myself over the moon in love with a wonderful woman and an opportunity to grow even farther as an Art Director and Creative Director. I gave my notice in Denver and moved out to California. I landed a great job as Creative Director for a mid-sized toy design company in Los Angeles, and I got married to the partner I had always dreamed of.

I was in The Flow, and California was my new, artistic canvas.

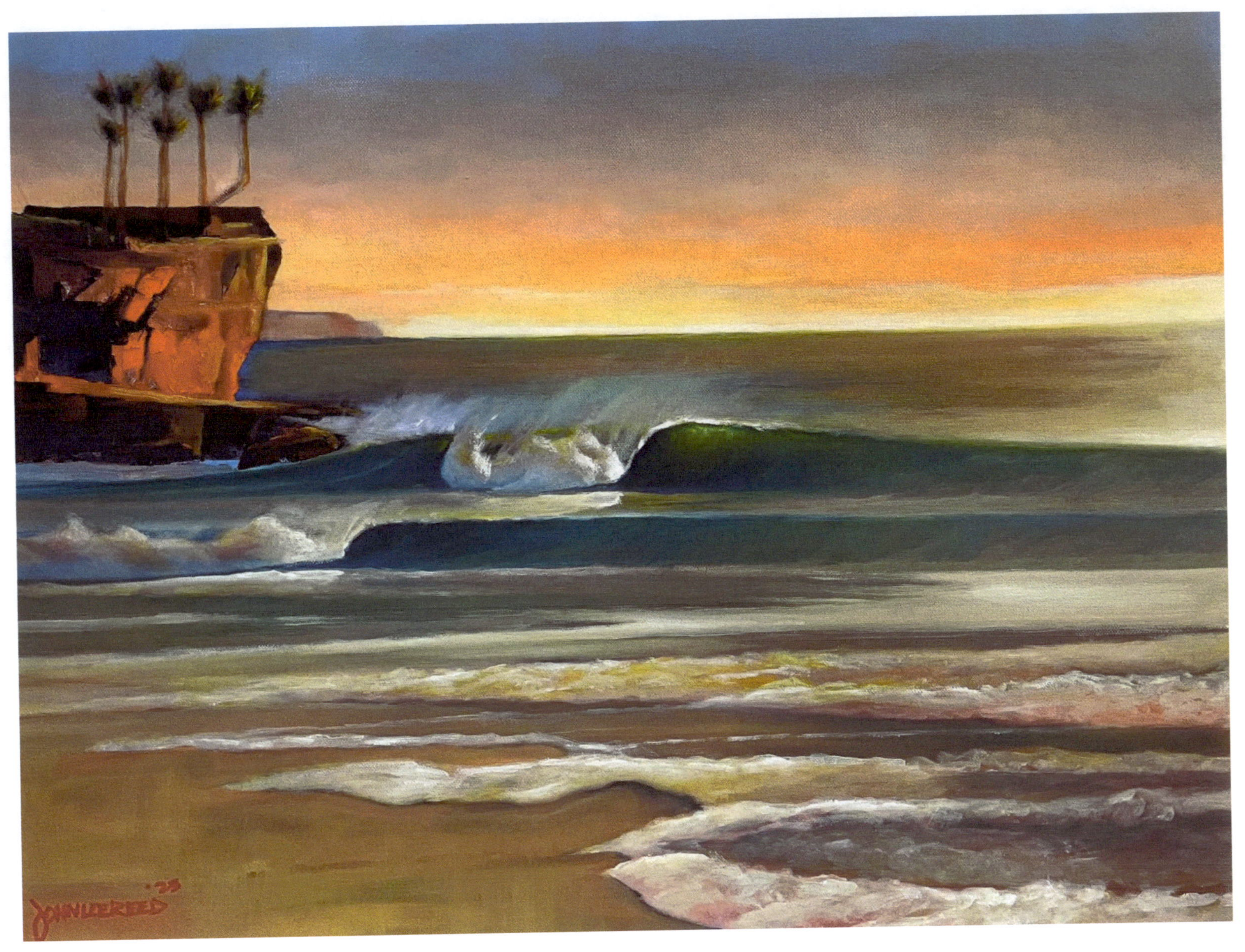

"Two Lefts Past Sunset" Oil on Canvas

The dramatic beauty of the beaches of Southern California had me awestruck. The surf pumped on a regular, consistent basis, much different from the beaches I had grown up on. The beauty of the California sunset would provide a creative quest that I would try to capture for the rest of my life. It also reminded me of how much God loves to paint and who the true Master really is.

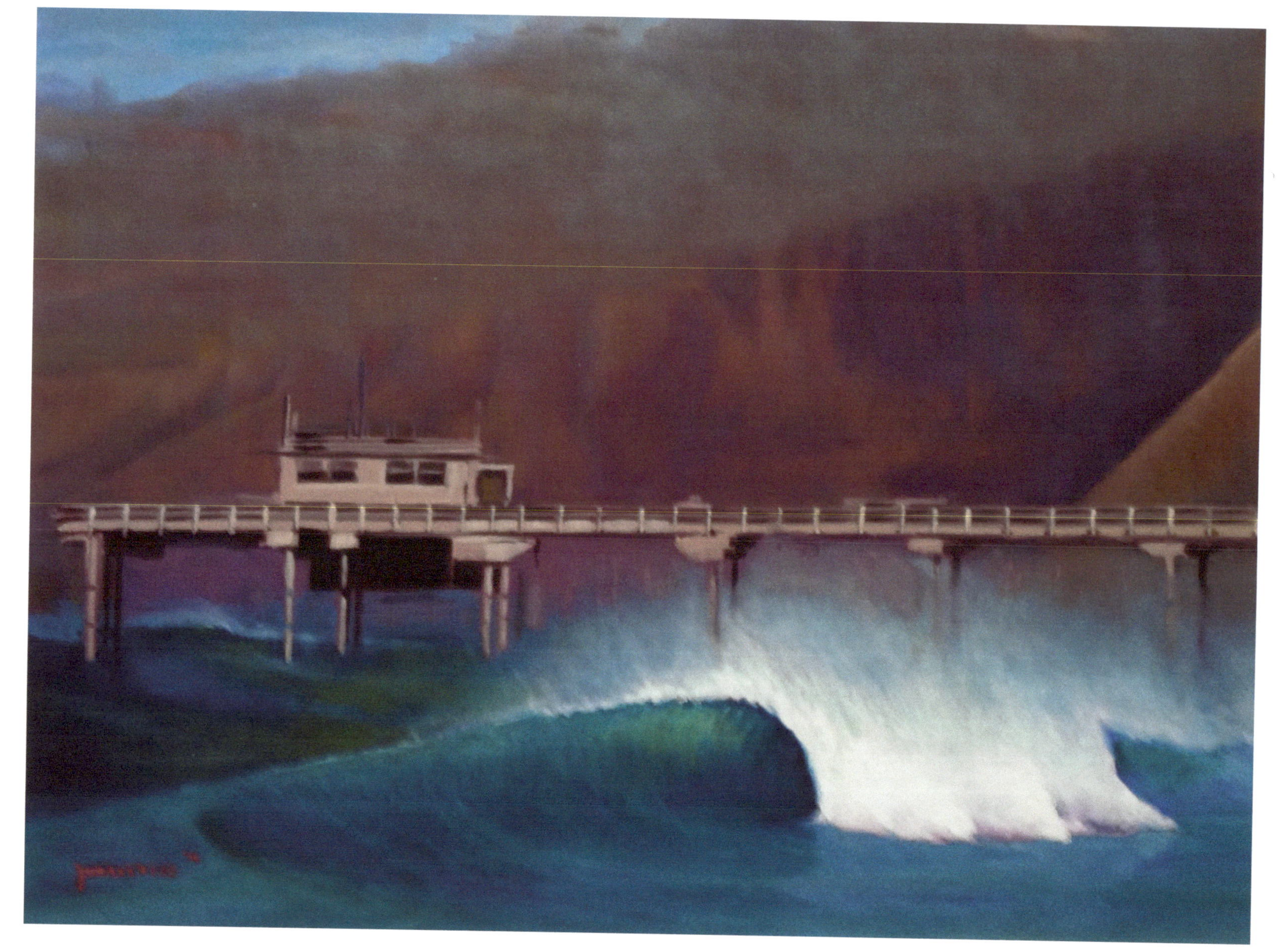

"Scripps Pier" Oil on Canvas

I did my best to surf and explore all the famous breaks in Southern California, from "Old Mans" to "Trestles," "Malibu," to "Ventura County Line." Each one had a different set of challenges and provided a unique test of my athletic ability and stamina. I met some great people in the local lineups, and I felt totally blessed to be playing on the famous playgrounds that we had only dreamed of growing up on the East Coast.

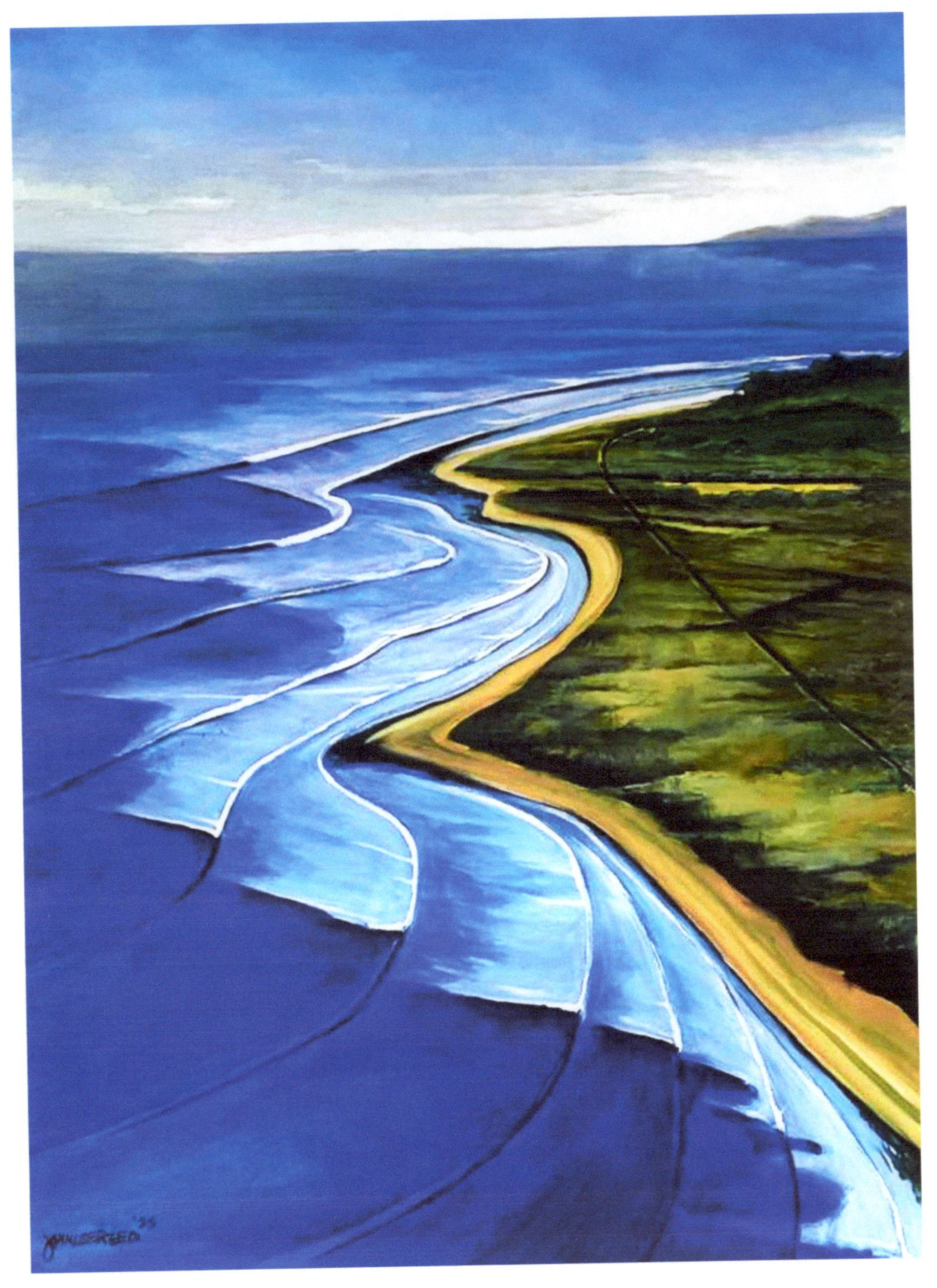

"Trestles Firing" Oil on Canvas

Famous, Southern California surf breaks like this one, offered up playgrounds that I had only dreamed of.

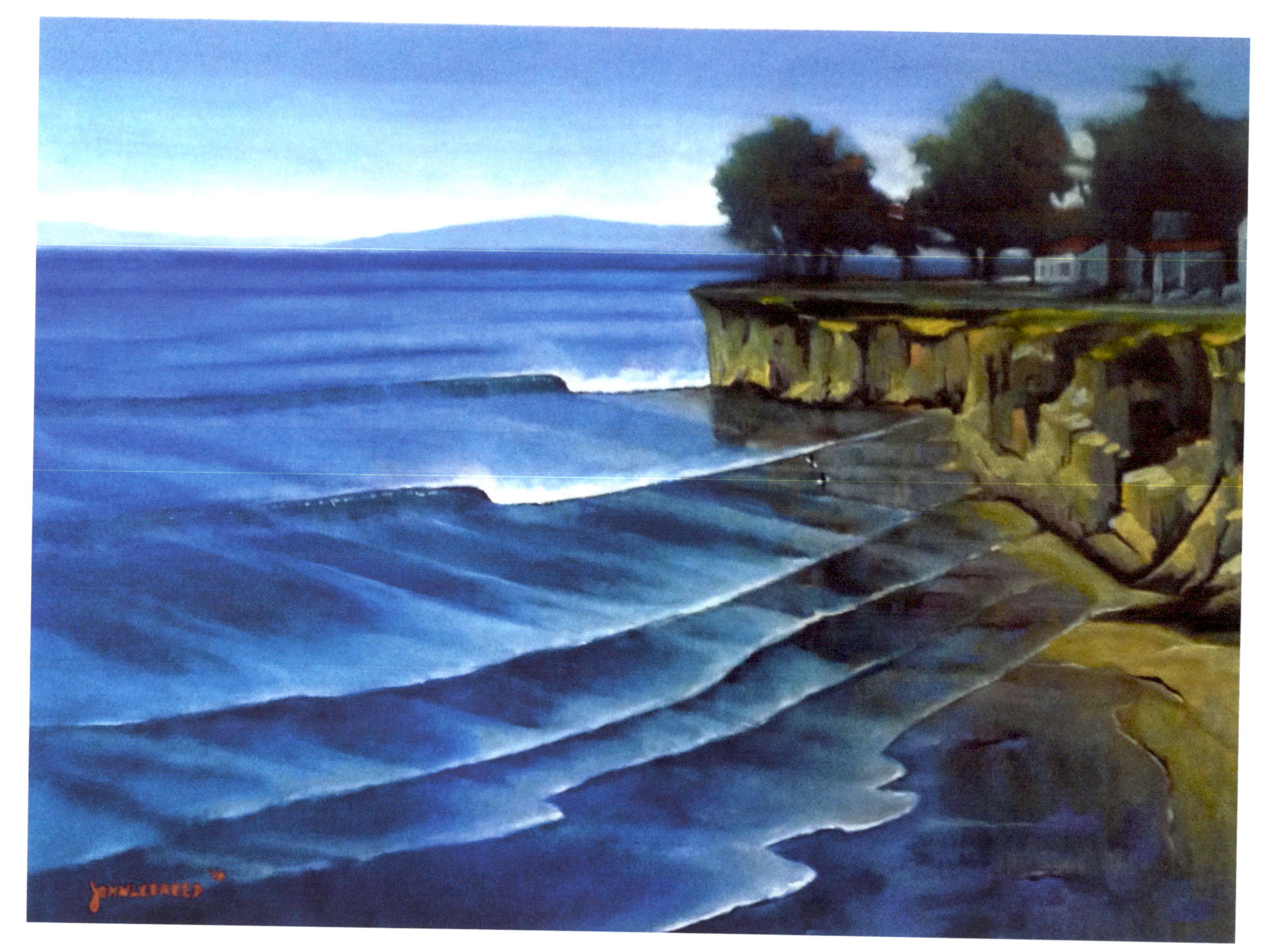

"Pleasure Point (Santa Cruz)" Oil on Canvas

The more I explored, the more I wanted to check out the new playgrounds that my adventure had to offer. Soon I was off to Northern Cal, Costa Rica, and other destinations to see and explore the beaches of my dreams.

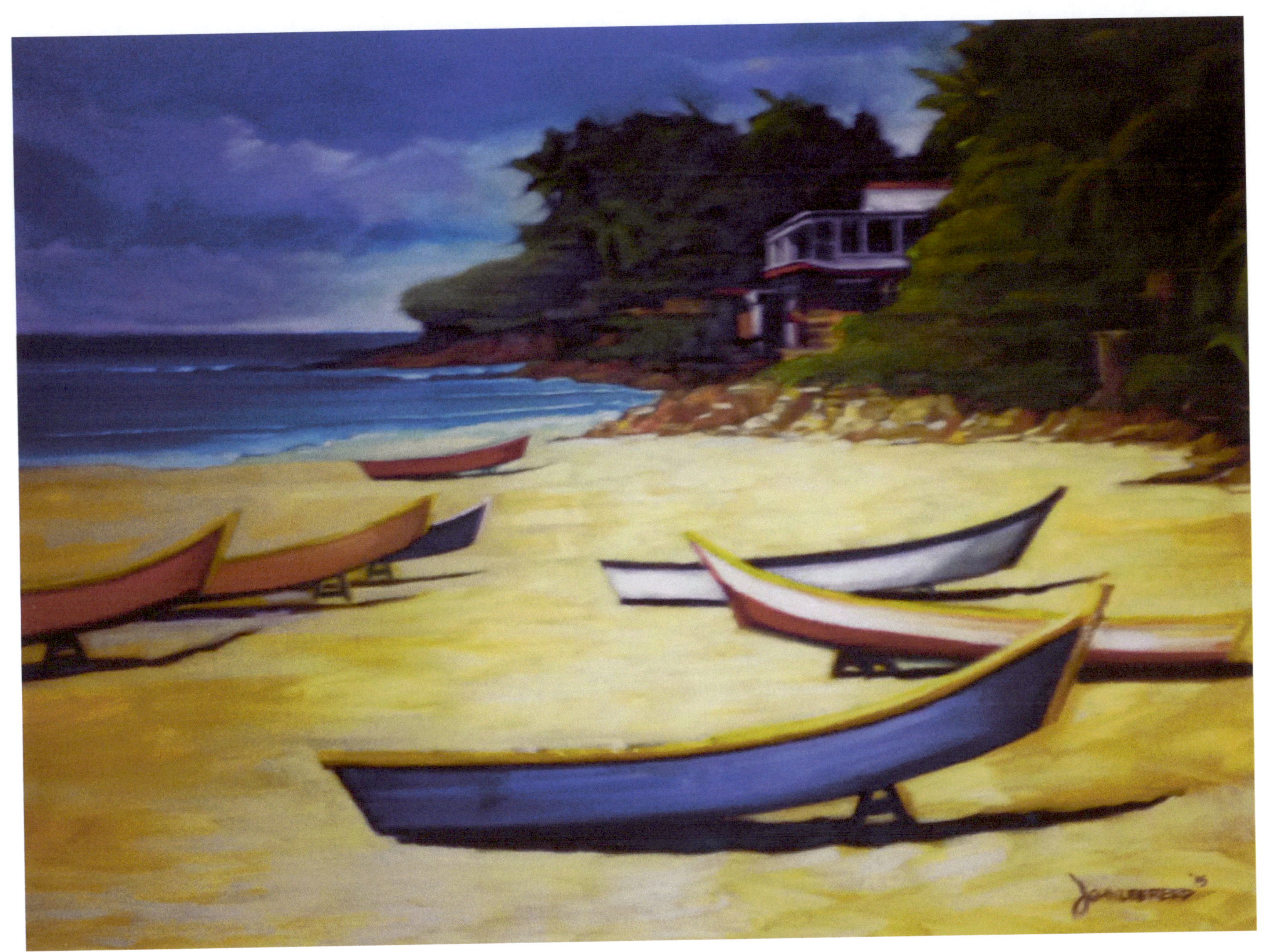

"Crash Boats (Puerto Rico)" Oil on Canvas (Photo Ref. Al Fisher)

Destination after destination provided wonderful reference for my art. My friends were also traveling the world surfing and sending me great photos of their favorite beaches to paint.

Balancing Priorities

Life, however, isn't just a continuous surf trip. My personal appreciation of God's Creation had to be balanced by a commitment to work and family. Luckily, I loved all three playgrounds, and the achievement of that balance is what makes everything work.

Along came three wonderful kids. The first two in a set and the third one all on her own.

Priorities and perspectives immediately changed our focus from individual pursuits to those that best suited the family unit.

I have never been more blessed. Being a father is the best job (and maybe the toughest) that I've ever taken on. Our little family was the focus of all our attention, and when the world changed on **September 11th, 2001**, we had to change with it.

I was driving to work that morning from Pacific Palisades into Beverly Hills when my wife called me on my car phone. She had the twins in a hotel room in Santa Monica after an HVAC worker stepped on a PVC pipe in our ceiling and burst it, sending hundreds of gallons of water into our beautiful, little hillside home. The twin babies were only a few months old.

"You're not going to believe what is on TV right now!" she said to me.

It was enough that she had to deal with two newborns in a new environment away from our comfortable home. Now, the disturbing confusion around the attack on our country was making things very difficult to understand and harder to handle. I continued to work that day, but Los Angeles was never the same. Like everyone in the country, we were on needles and pins about what might happen next. New York and Washington D.C. had been attacked, and we had every reason to be wary that LA could be next. We tried our best to keep our composure, but our newly formed parental instincts had taken a hit, just like the Towers of The World Trade Center.

Two nights later, while sleeping in our room on the 14th floor of the Santa Monica Hotel, we were awakened in the middle of the night by a magnitude 5.3 earthquake that rattled the windows and made the building sway back and forth like a Hollywood palm tree in the August Santa Annas.

Strike three. We didn't know if we wanted to raise our children in LA anyway. We decided to listen to The Flow and start looking for a new place in California that we could call home.

We turned the boat and headed North.

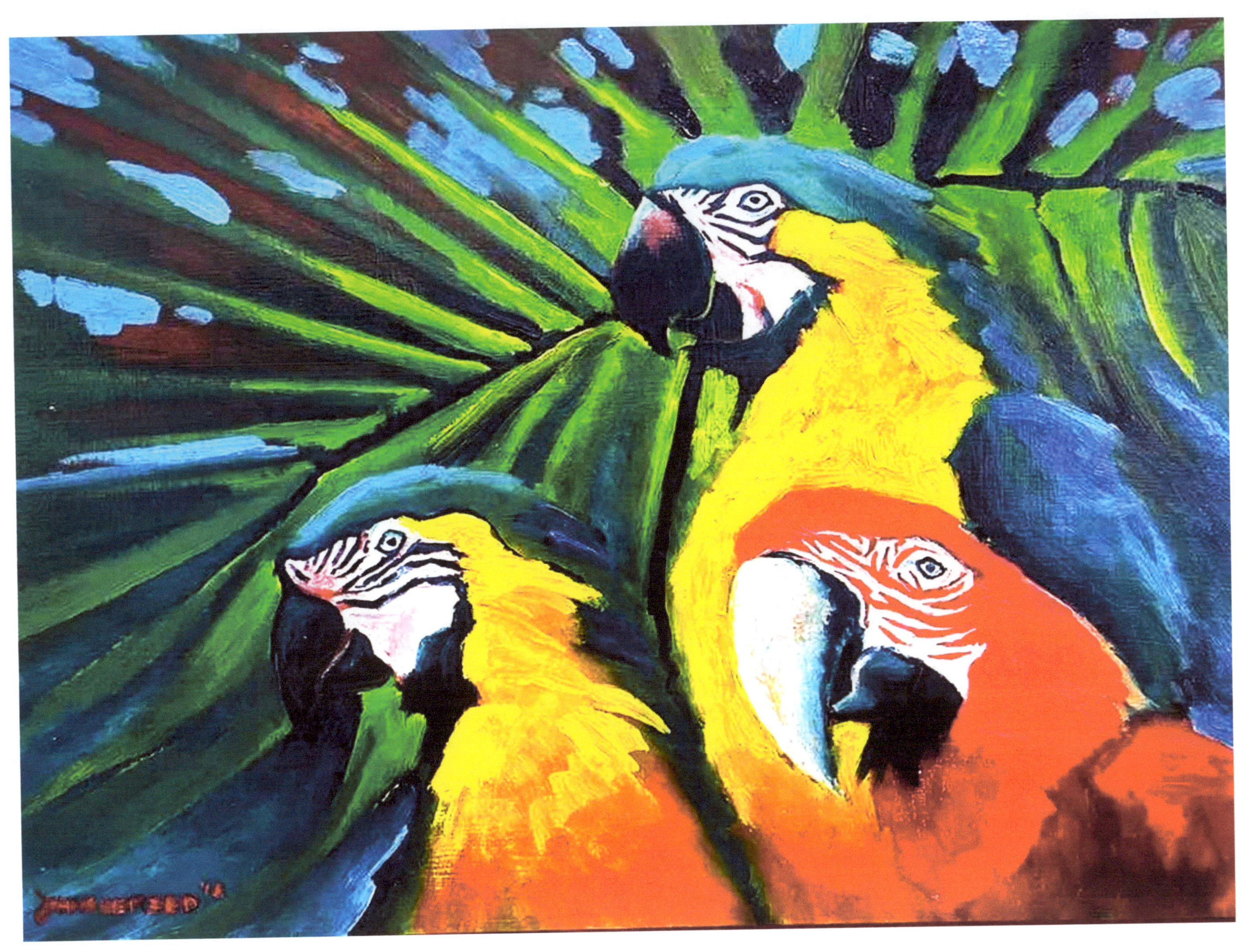

"Three Stooges" Oil on Canvas

When the littles came along, my perspective changed once again. They are challenging, but boy, are they colorful!

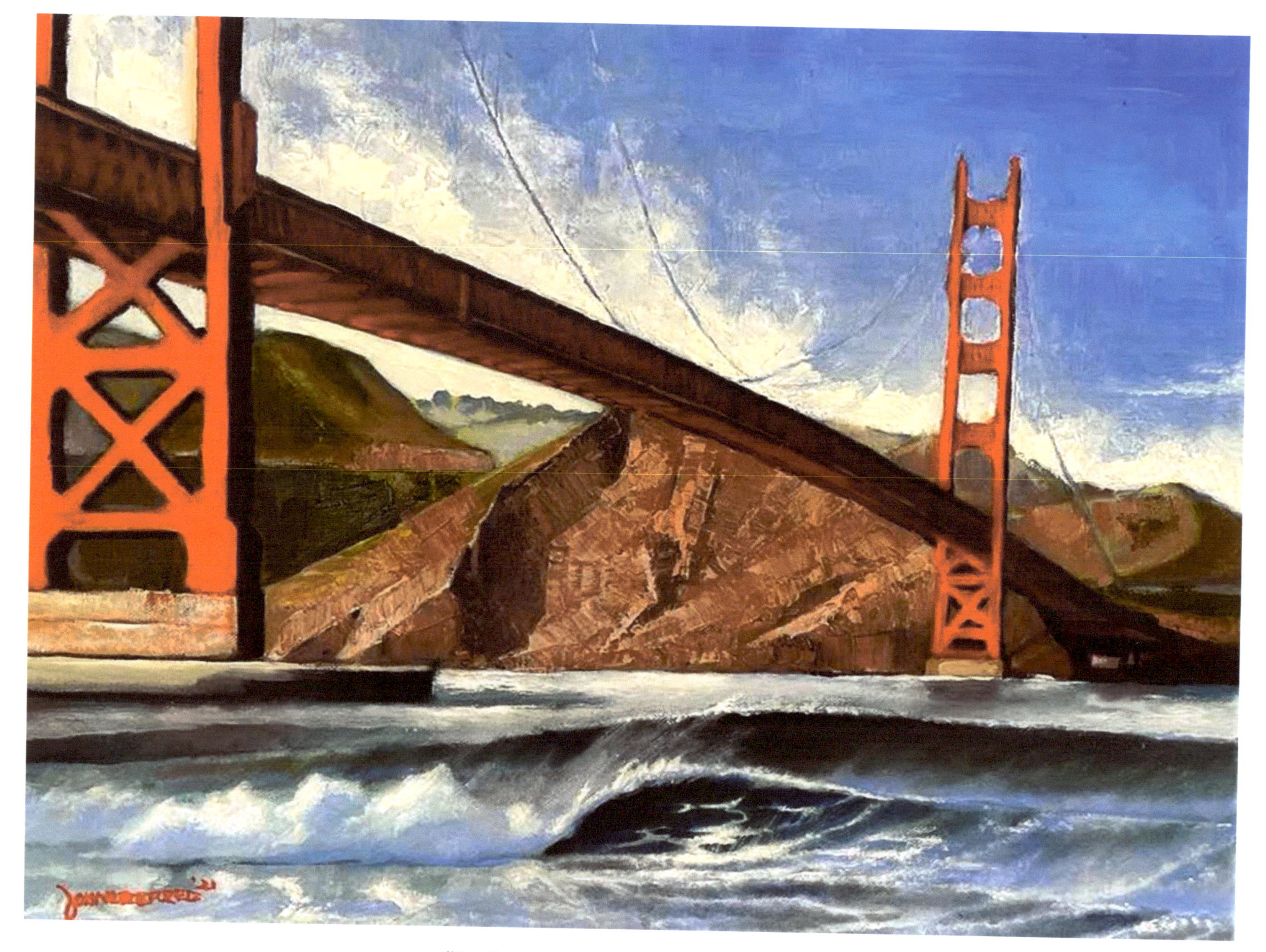

"Surf SF (Fort Point)" Oil on Canvas

Home to the 5MM wetsuit and "The Man in the Grey Suit," Northern California surfing was
filled with its own unique challenges.

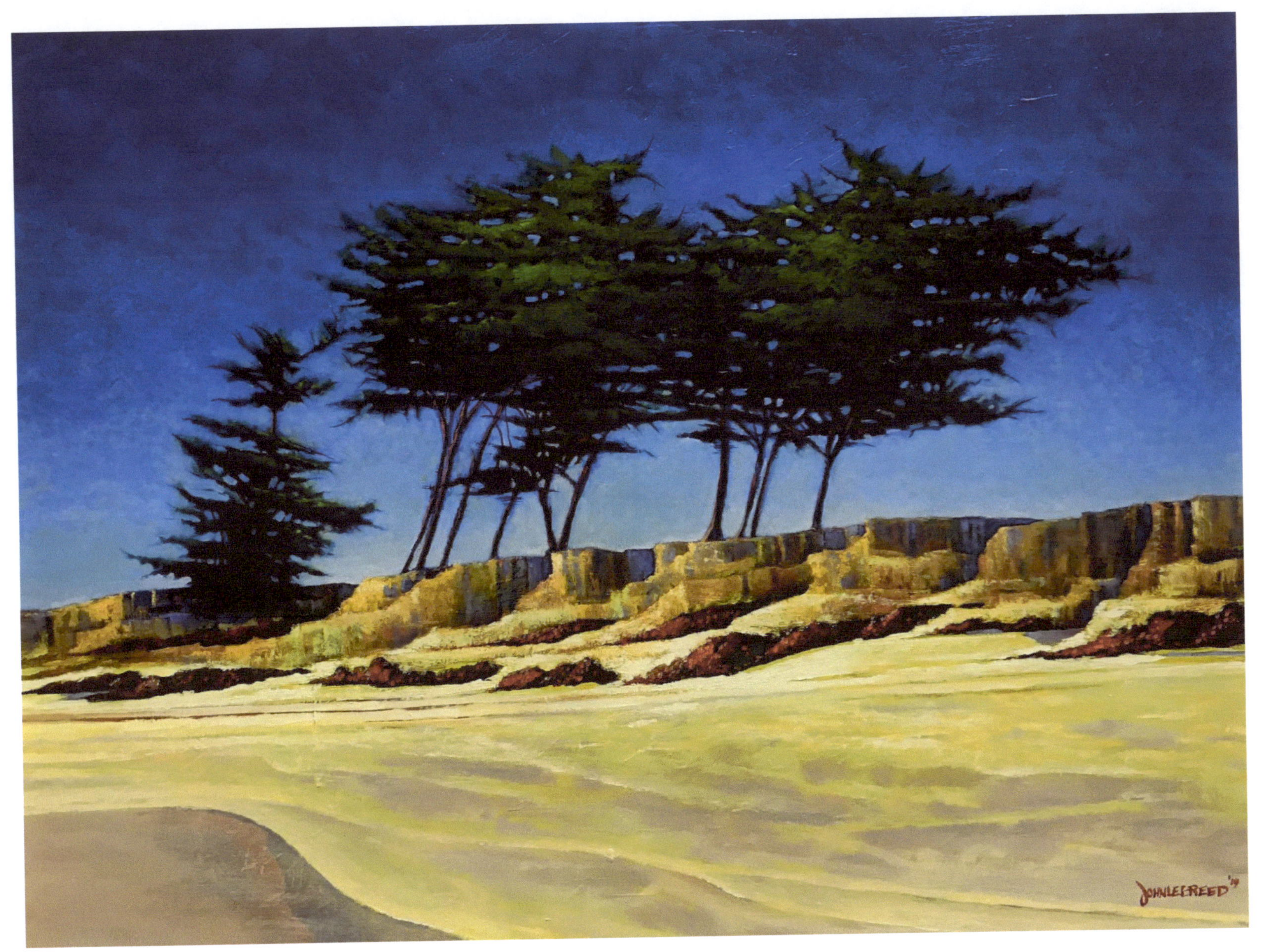

"Fort Bragg Cliffs" Oil on Canvas

The coastline in the North is breathtakingly beautiful. The scarcity of consistent, warm sunshine makes it much different than the beaches in the southern part of the state, but those characteristics are what give it its charm. As the family grew and I began to paint with much more consistency, I often searched for isolated coastlines to satisfy my desire for photographic reference.

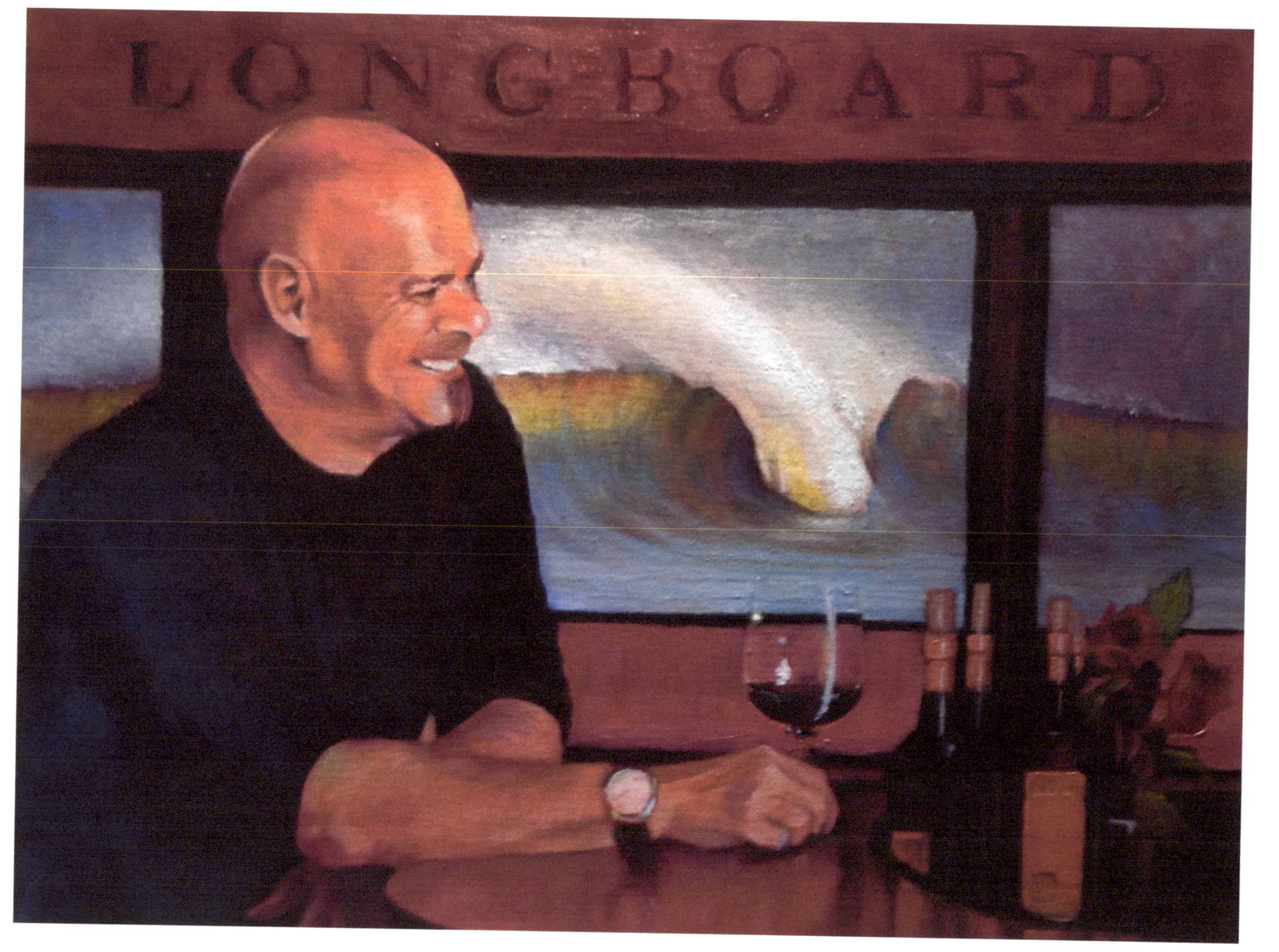

"Oded" Oil on Canvas

The California Wine Country was where we settled in to raise our young family. We grew wine grapes for several years on a few different pieces of Sonoma County property. Getting to know some of the players in the industry was an amazing experience. I even got to know one of the best winemakers in the region, who just happens to be a dedicated surfer. Oded Shakked, owner and winemaker at Longboard Vineyards, allowed me to display some of my art in the winery and even create his portrait, which hangs on the wall in the tasting area, still today.

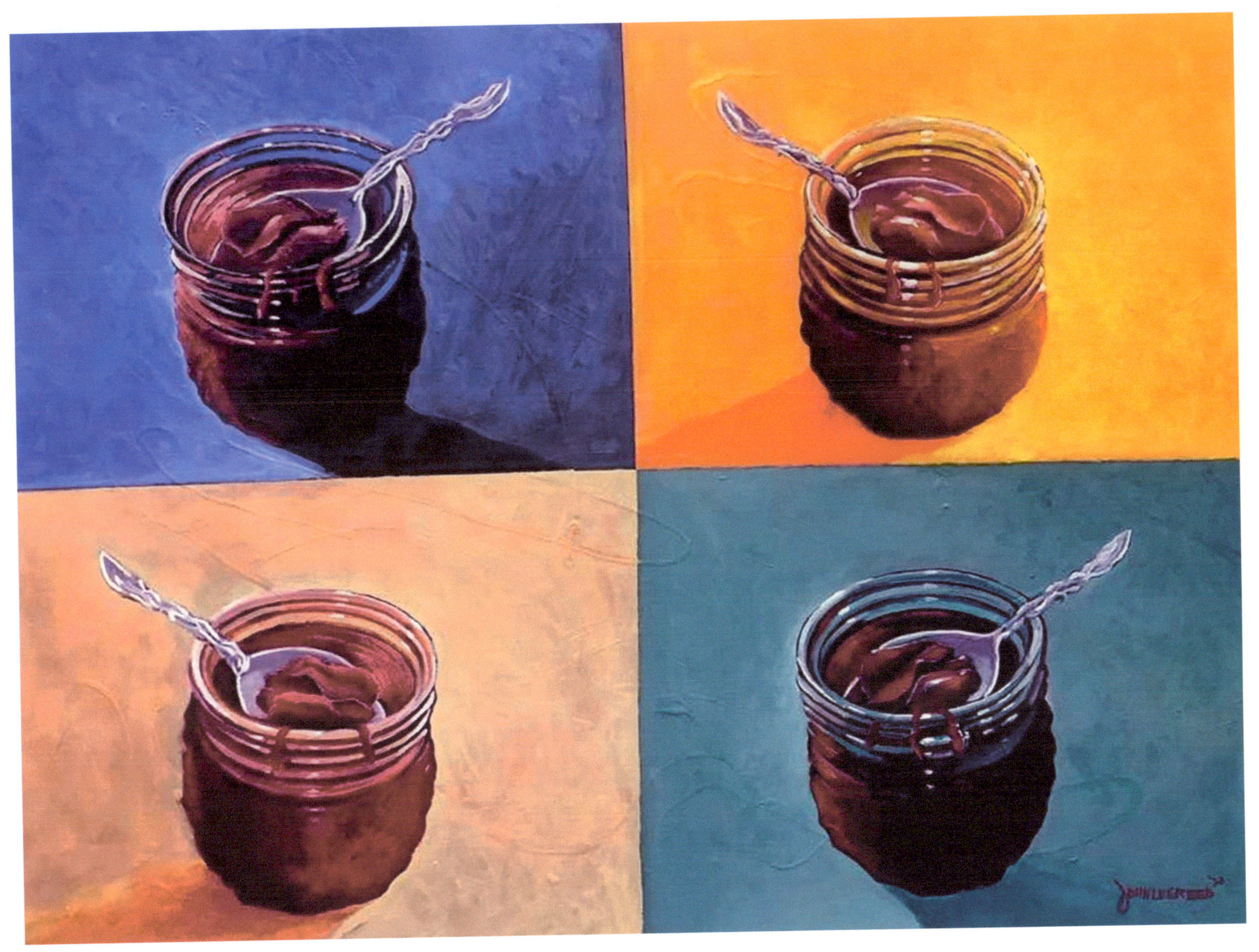

"We Jammin'" Oil on Canvas

I created several pieces of art for wineries across the county, and it was always a challenge to come up with something that wasn't just a vineyard landscape. This large piece hangs in my buddy's tasting room as a reminder to your palate of his "jammy" tasting Pinot Noir.

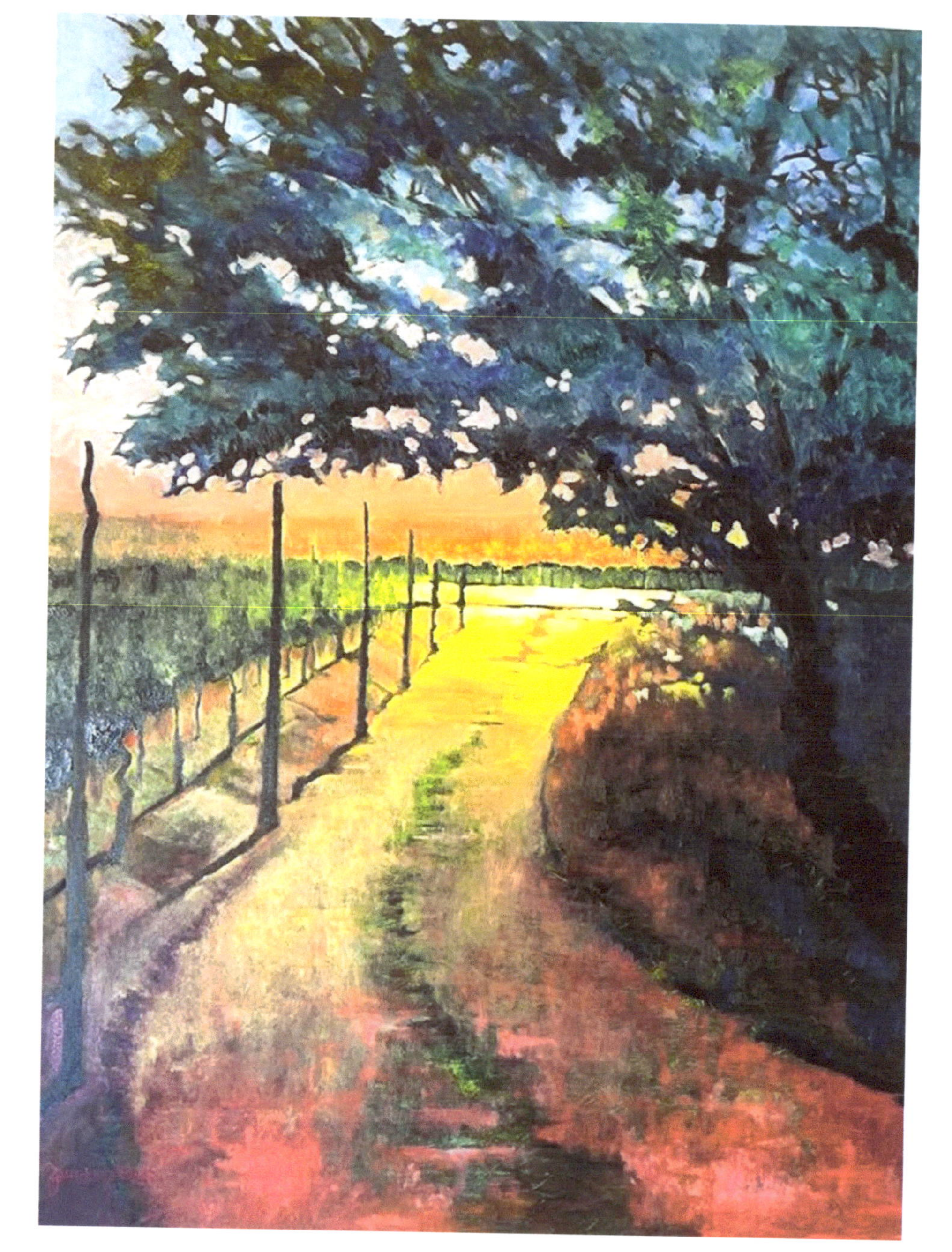

"Vineyard Run" Oil on Canvas

The blazing colors of the post-harvest vineyards in Sonoma County were nothing short of spectacular.

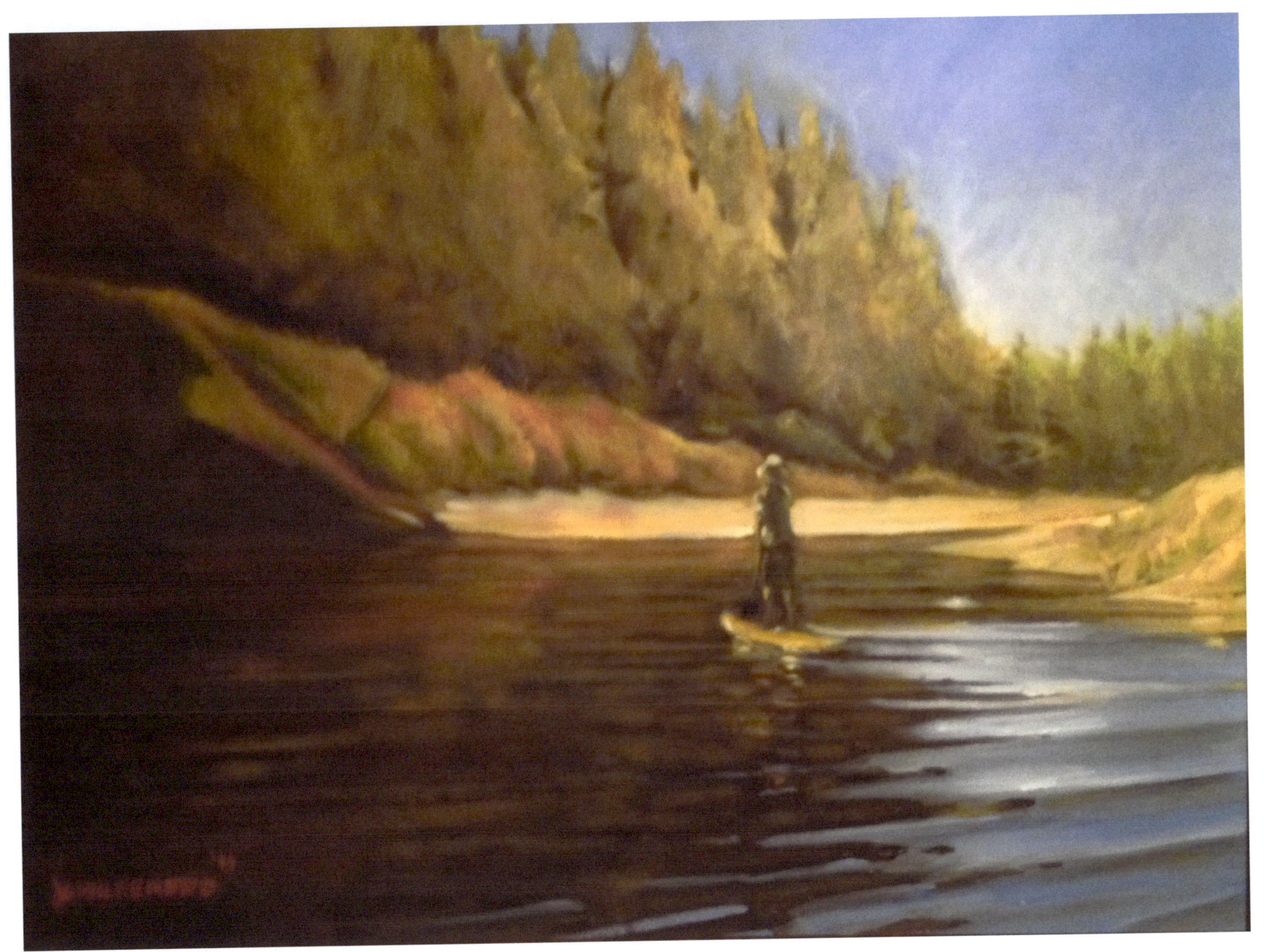

"Russian River Paddle" Oil on Canvas

The great Russian River flowed through our town to the Pacific Ocean, providing us with unmatched beauty and great paddling adventure.

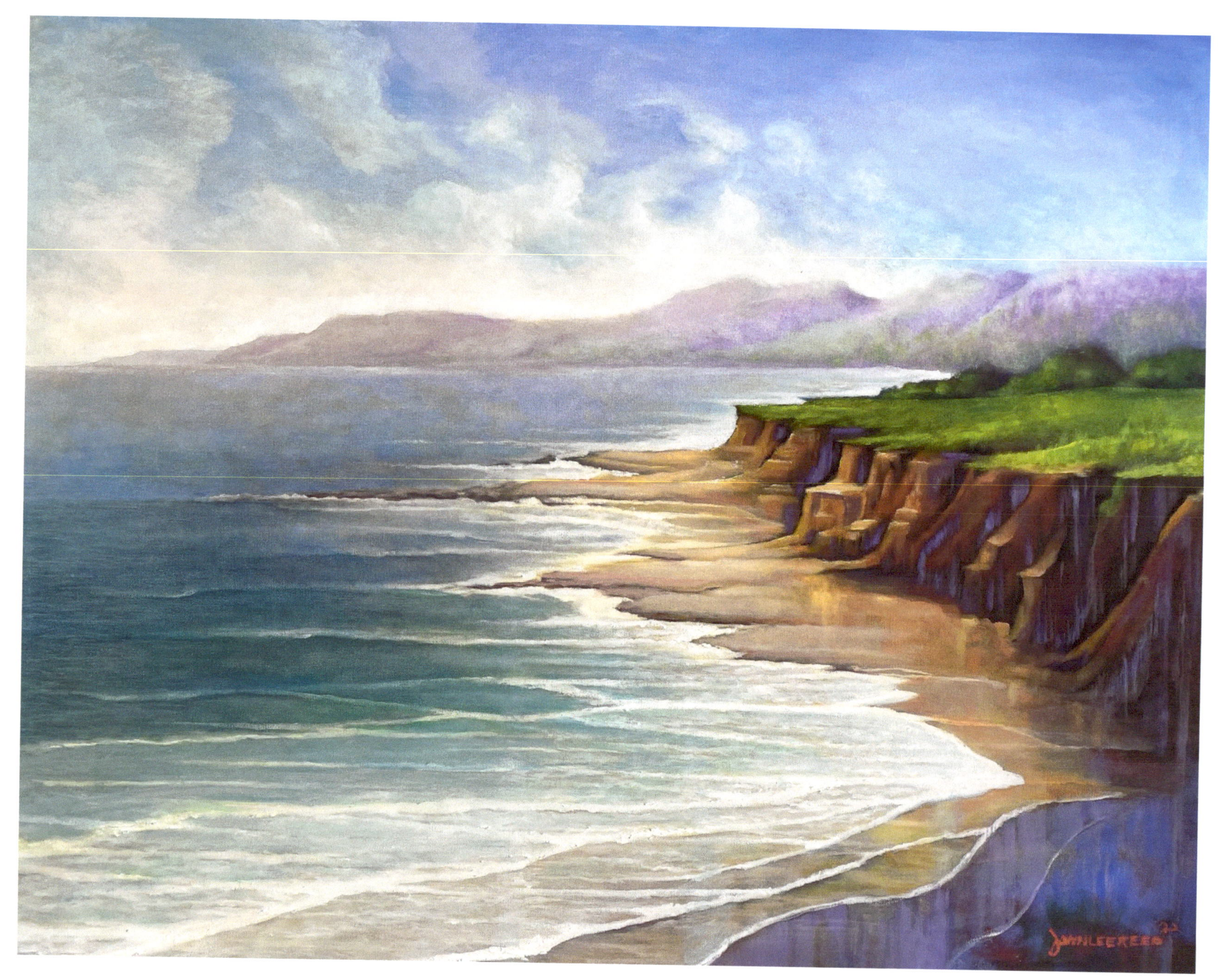

"Cali Cliffs" Oil on Canvas

The rugged and dramatic coastline of Northern California provided endless artistic reference for me.

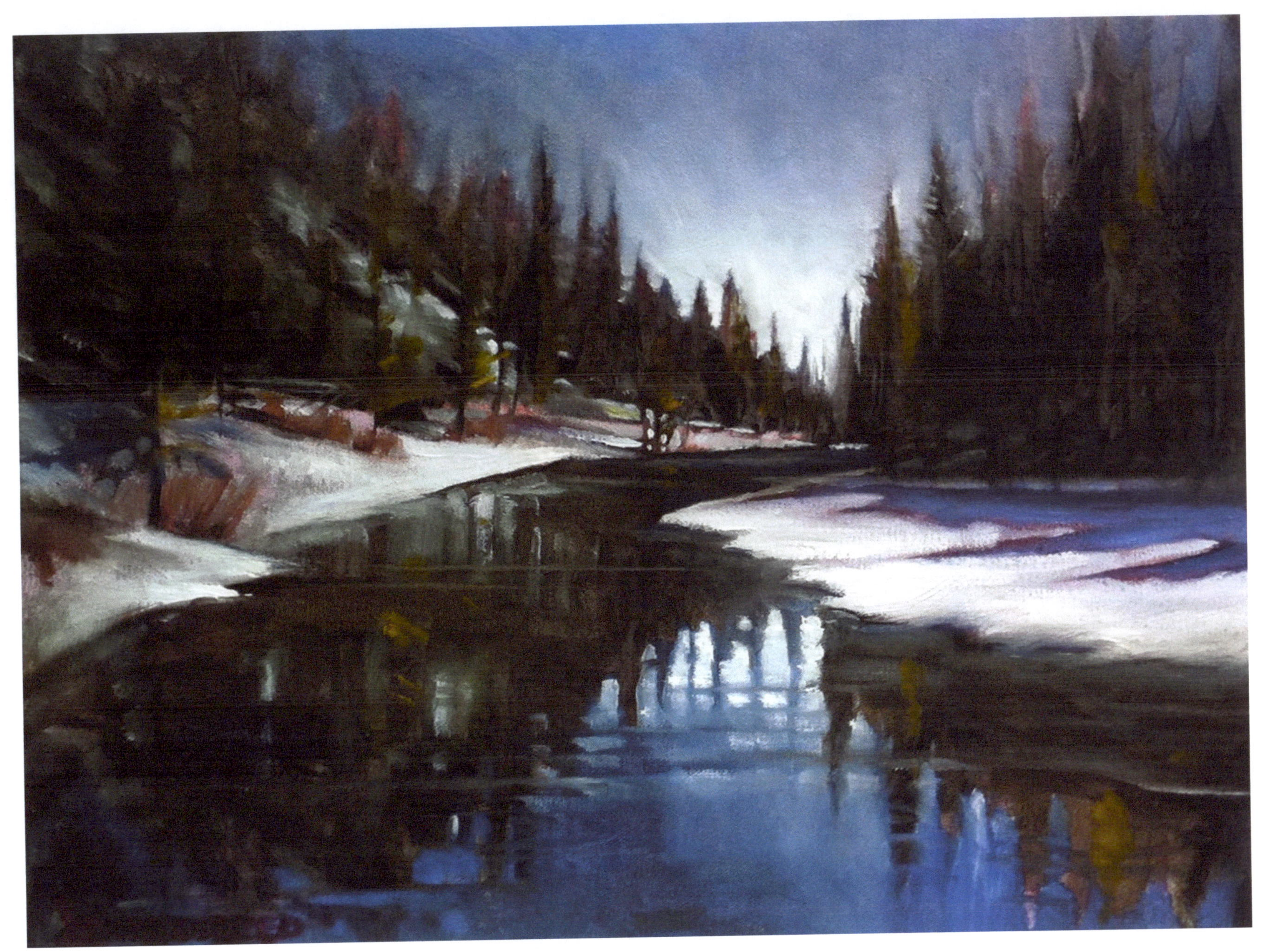

"Truckee River" Oil on Canvas

Pushing away from the coast, Lake Tahoe and the surrounding beauty of the High Sierra also provided ample creative reference for my continuing education.

Travel

There's a wide and wonderful world out there. Go get it, baby!

One of the great things about surfing is that from an early age; it pushes you to travel.

Just like Bruce Brown's iconic film 'Endless Summer" surfers across the planet are always searching for the next perfect wave. There is however, more to learn from your travels than just who has the best point break or the longest, most consistent left-hander (though I get it that some of you might argue that point!)

Yes, traveling, especially with a family, costs money. It does.

So, work your tail off when you are working and put some of that doe-ray-me away so that you can take the family unit and go explore different places across the planet. Later in life, you'll remember the adventures, not the costs involved.

We hiked up the kids and took them out of school for lots of different excursions. If you can, do it while they are younger because, by the time they get to be teenagers, the only way you'll be able to make them happy is by dragging (and paying for) a couple of their friends along with you!

Even then, it's completely worth it.

There was always beach time factored into our excursions, but we also made every effort to get to know the local people in different places that we visited.

Remember, when you visit faraway lands, you are always a representative of perspective.

Just like The Quadrant says, 'Live Native". Talk to the locals and try to learn their local language. Find out about the stereotypes that they have around visitors to their part of the world and work to break down those barriers. You will leave the planet a better place if you do, and you'll also teach your children to look at the world from a broader perspective than simply their own.

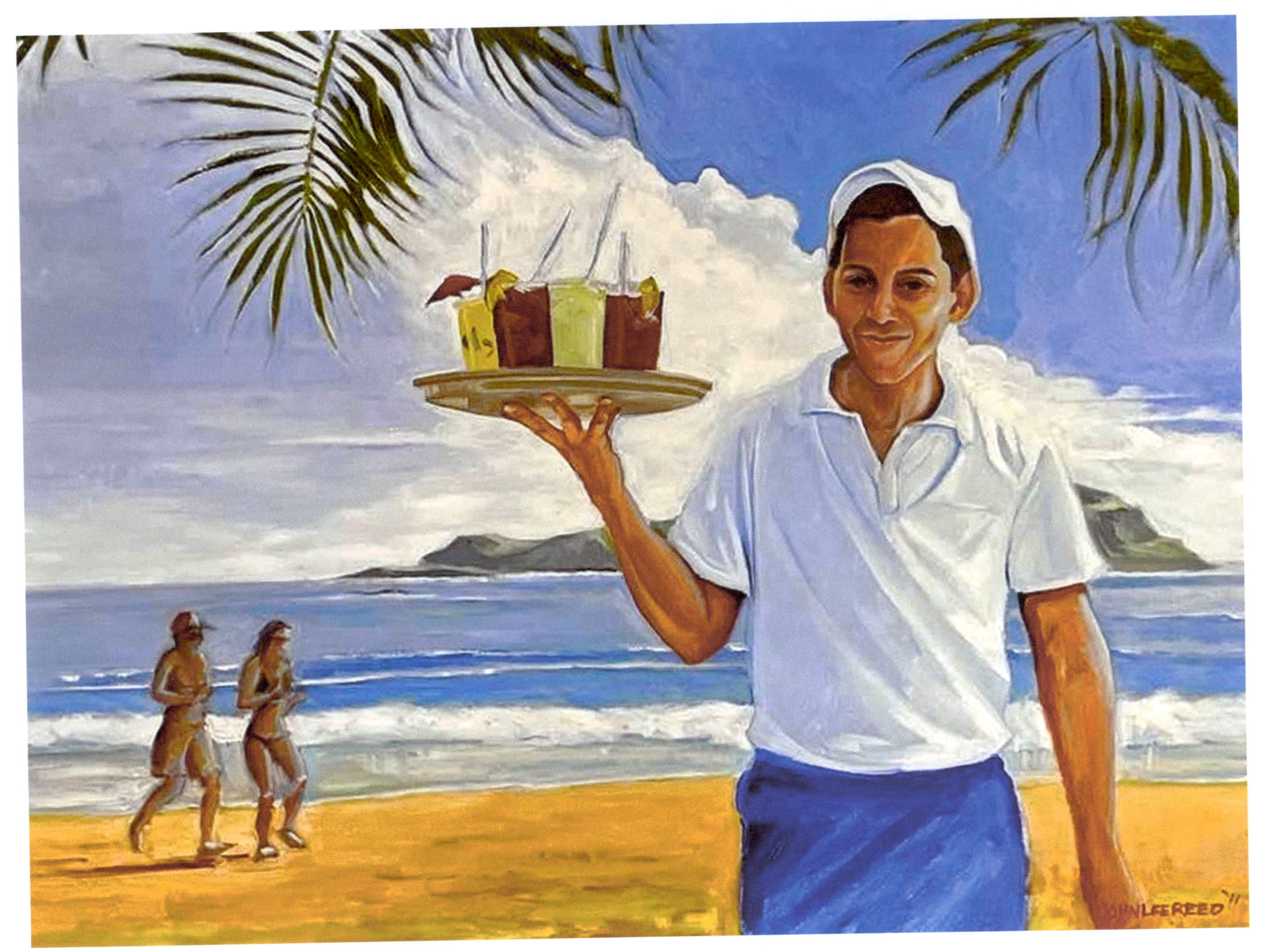

"(I guess we can run) Manana" Oil on Canvas

Whenever we traveled, I always made sure that I got my running and physical workouts in. Some days however, were just made for kicking back and relaxing.

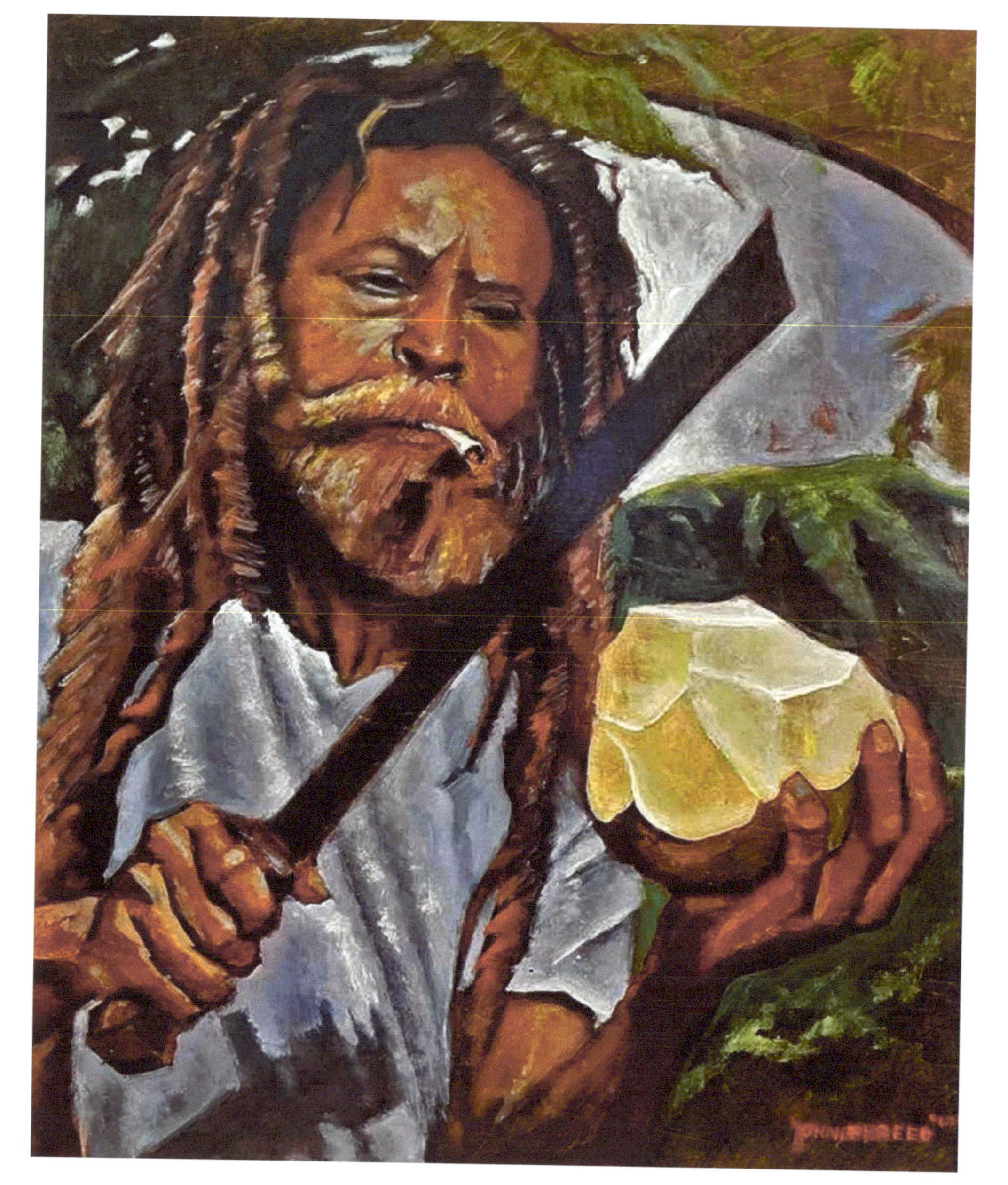

"CoCoNut Man" Oil on Birch Panel

We were able to travel and take the kids to Hawaii, Jamaica and other islands as they were growing up and I always did my best to hunt for great photographic references along the way. The local people in the islands have always captured my imagination.

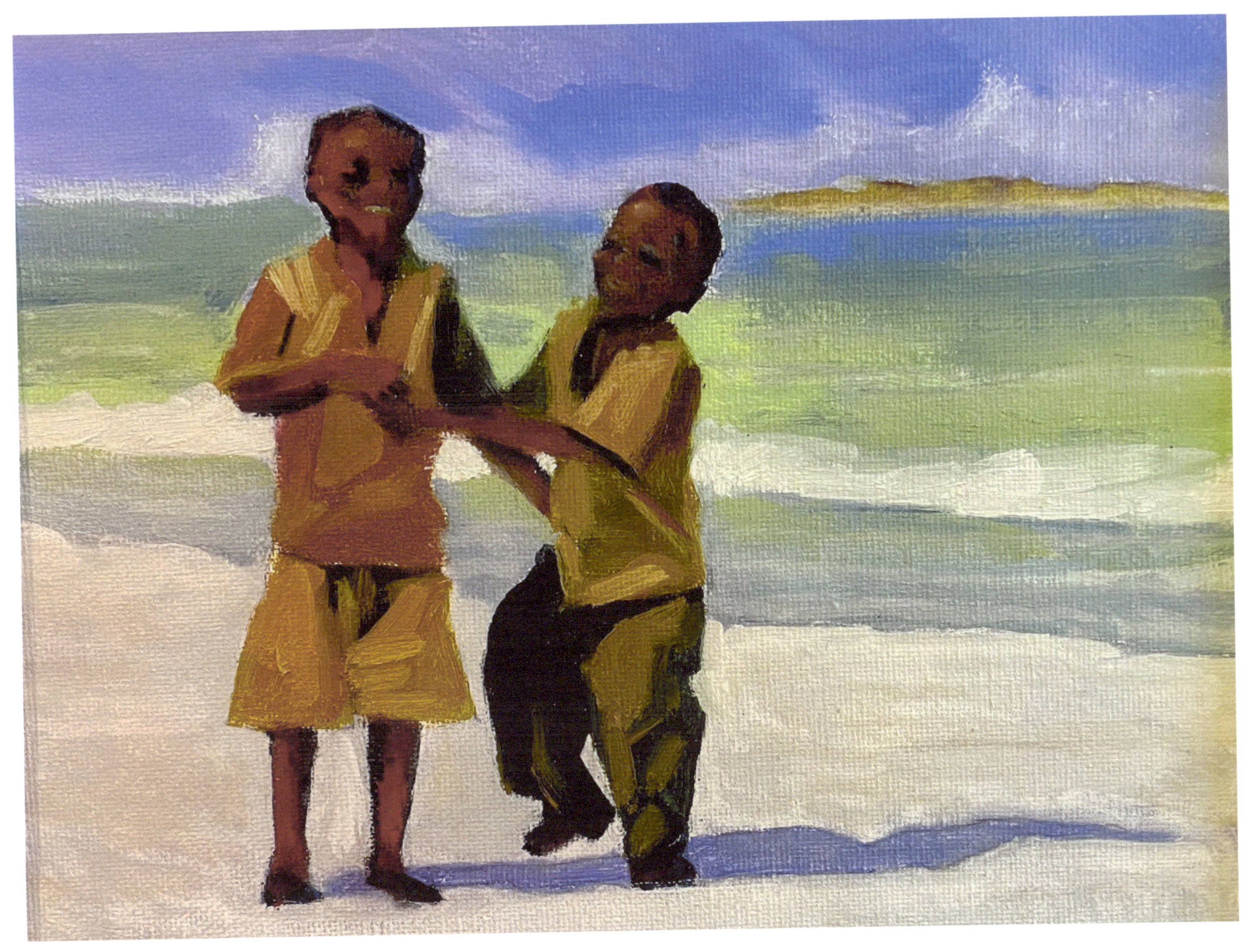

"Local Littles" Oil on Canvas

Island life has a simple joy that is expressly evident on the faces of the local kids. These two don't need a cell phone or a new pair of Air Jordans to be happy, and that is just the way they roll. My goal in this quick sketch was to try to capture that joy with a minimal amount of brush strokes and tight detail. The looseness of this little painting makes it one of my favorites.

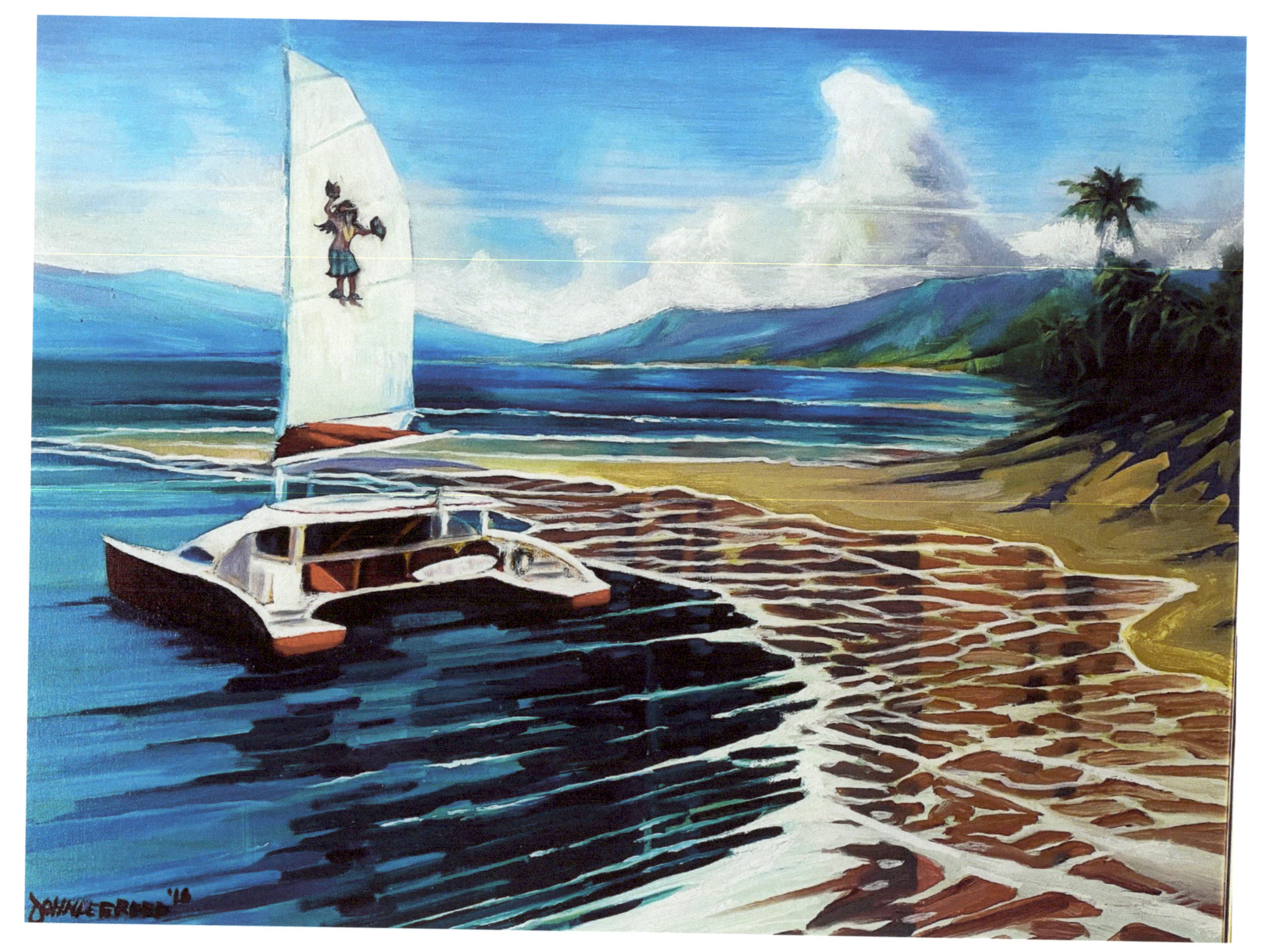

"Island Anchor" Oil on Canvas

Sometimes I like to simply push the outside of the envelope by using color and contrast to express how I feel about a certain place or moment in time. Call it my 'mushroom style' if you will, but it's always fun to venture away from the challenge of realism and let go with an expression of vibrance and color.

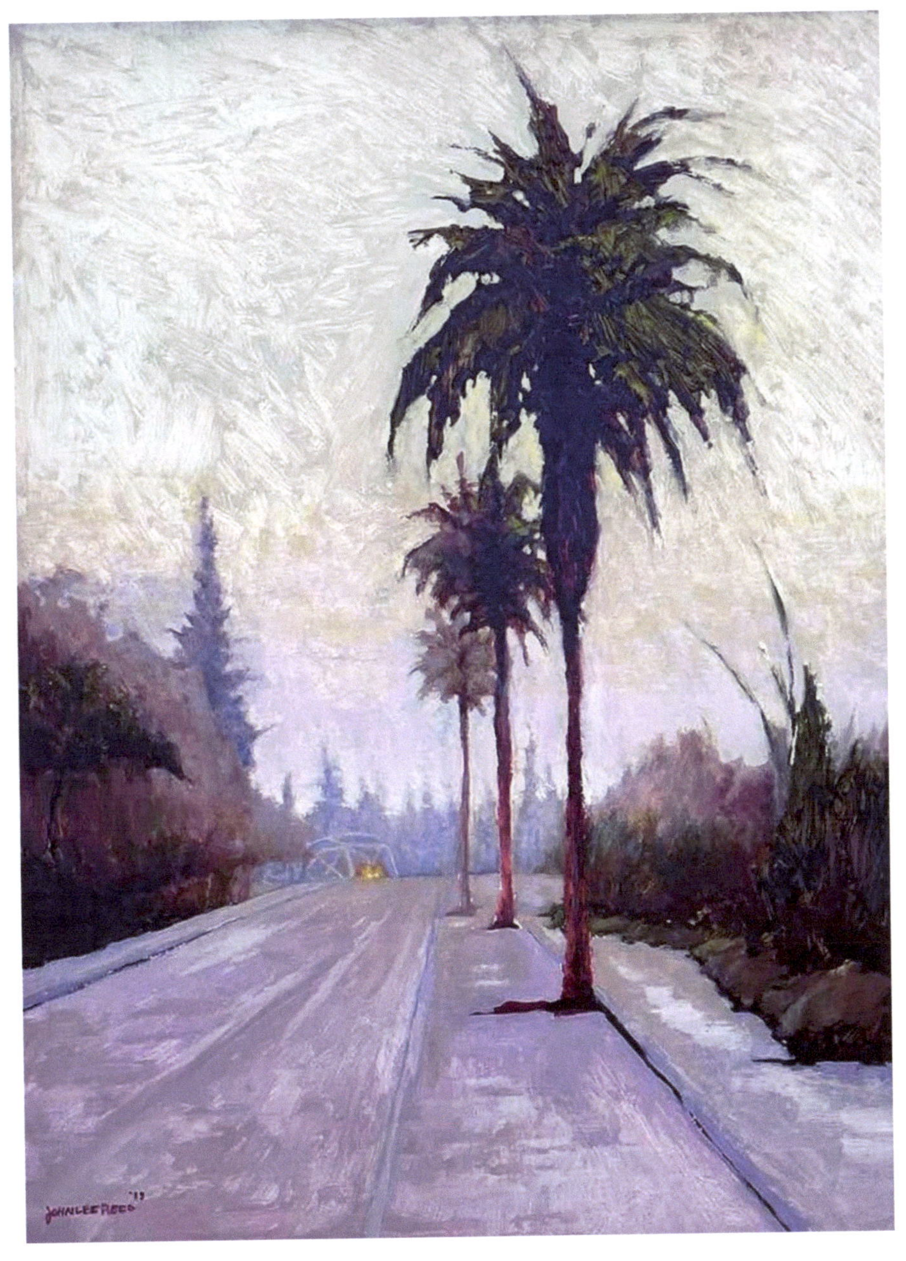

"The Road Outta H Town" Oil on Canvas

Throughout our travels, we were lucky to call Northern Cal our home base. It was a wonderful place to raise a family and it provided me with ample creative opportunity as an artist. I am truly blessed to have had the amazing journey that I have had, dancing along in the Flow of The Universe.

Standing in Gratitude

Many people ask me about my "influences" as an artist.

I tell them that I have many heroes that have influenced my work both directly and indirectly over the years. Those heroes, for me, mainly come from the school of Illustration, more so than from what academics call "Fine Art." My feeling, however, is that there is no discernable difference between the two.

Are you going to tell me that N.C. Wyeth, Maxfield Parrish, and Norman Rockwell were not Artists!? Those cats were Rock Stars!

That's like saying that Jimi Hendrix was not an innovative musician.

It just ain't true.

Surf Art, as we know it today, arose in the 1960s as surfing culture swept its way from the California Coast to the East Coast and beyond. Publications like SURFER Magazine and rock and rollers like The Beach Boys introduced our hungry, East Coast imaginations to the new vibration of surfing and surf culture. They were the ones that had us young, Right Coasters dreaming of California. It was those dudes that had me drawing waves in my Algebra II notebooks when I was supposed to be memorizing equations and solving for X (whatever that means).

Artists like Rick Griffin and Bill Ogden hooked us with stunningly colorful characters and images of amazing, perfect surf breaks on the lost islands of our imaginations. Posters began to surface for underground surf films made by Bruce Brown and Jim Freeman. Growing up in the late '60s and early 70's, we "Groms" were the benefactors of a cultural revolution that defined our music, dress, way of speaking, and certainly our artwork.

For that, I stand in total gratitude (dude)!

Hey, I have an overwhelming and classic appreciation for artists like Michelangelo, Rembrandt van Rijn, Paul Gauguin, John Singer Sargent, Diego Velasquez, and Joaquin Sorolla. Those guys certainly created the benchmarks for quality self-expression and reproduction using a brush and some pigments.

It was the early California Surf Artists, however, who made artwork too enticing not to "Go for it".

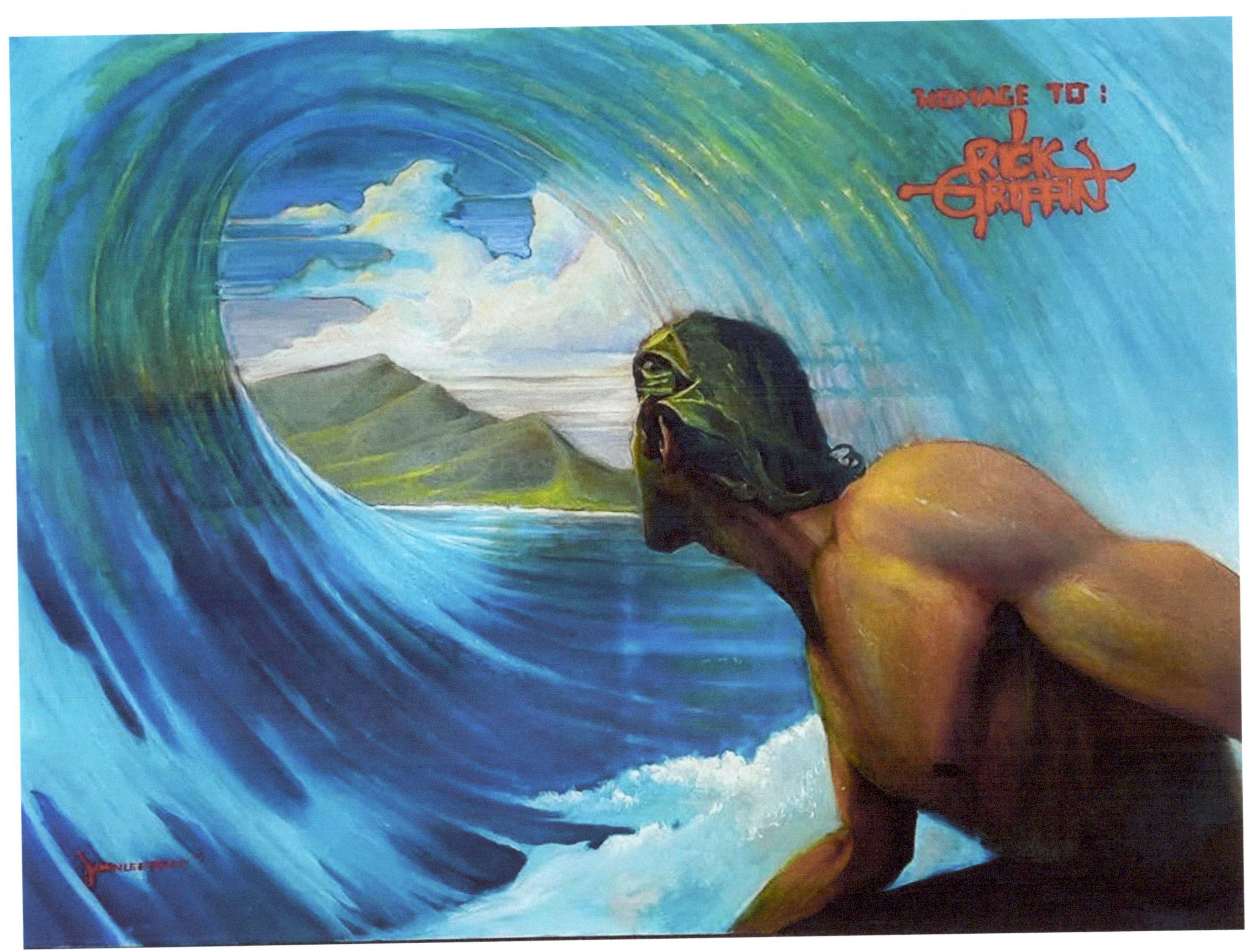

"Homage to Rick Griffin" Oil on Canvas

I painted this as an homage to my hero Rick Griffin. Rick did early artwork for SURFER magazine as well as other surfing-related characters and movie posters. His poster for the 1975 film "Tales from the Tube" inspired me like no other to want to create the Artwork of Surfing.

Acknowledgments

My first and foremost acknowledgment goes to the greatest painter ever in existence.

If you've ever marveled over an evening sunset or an early morning sunrise, you know to whom I refer. Call him God, Jesus, Allah, Buddha, or whatever name works for you. You may find it simpler, as I sometimes do, to refer to Him or Her simply as "The Universe."

I'm not here to debate you around that. In my opinion, you have every right to believe whatever you want to believe.

I am here to tell you, however, that you can reach out to The Universe, and that relationship can be a guiding light in your life. You simply need to find the part of the channel where the current flows the strongest for you and swim along in that direction.

There is a plan for you, and it includes all the success and abundance that The Universe has to offer. It's already in place, but, like Sister Agatha said to me, all you have to do is "not screw it up."

Many people have generously supported my artistic quest over the years, and I could not have done the work without them. Thank yous certainly go out to my brother-in-law Troy Lowrie who accepted me into his family and continued to stick with me through thick and thin.

Several of my cohorts who have supported me in this venture include my friends Bill Loftus, James McClenahan, Albert Fisher, Cris Timmons, Aaron Locks, Jen Lee Guthrie, Bruce Marquette, Tammra and Keith Borrall, Dennis Singleton and Dan and Alyson Dorr. Thank you, too, to Larry Butler for letting me sleep on the floor of his apartment for 3 months in Fort Lauderdale while I got started in Art School.

Certainly, thank yous go out to out to my children Zack, Kira, and Capri Reed. We will miss your mother every day but know that her presence will be felt through all of your many successes.

There are so many more people to mention. Please know that all of you have contributed to the development of this publication. If this little book, or for that matter, any one of us who experiences it, can help anyone find their way in life, then we all have found our flow.

Peace and Blessings,

JLR

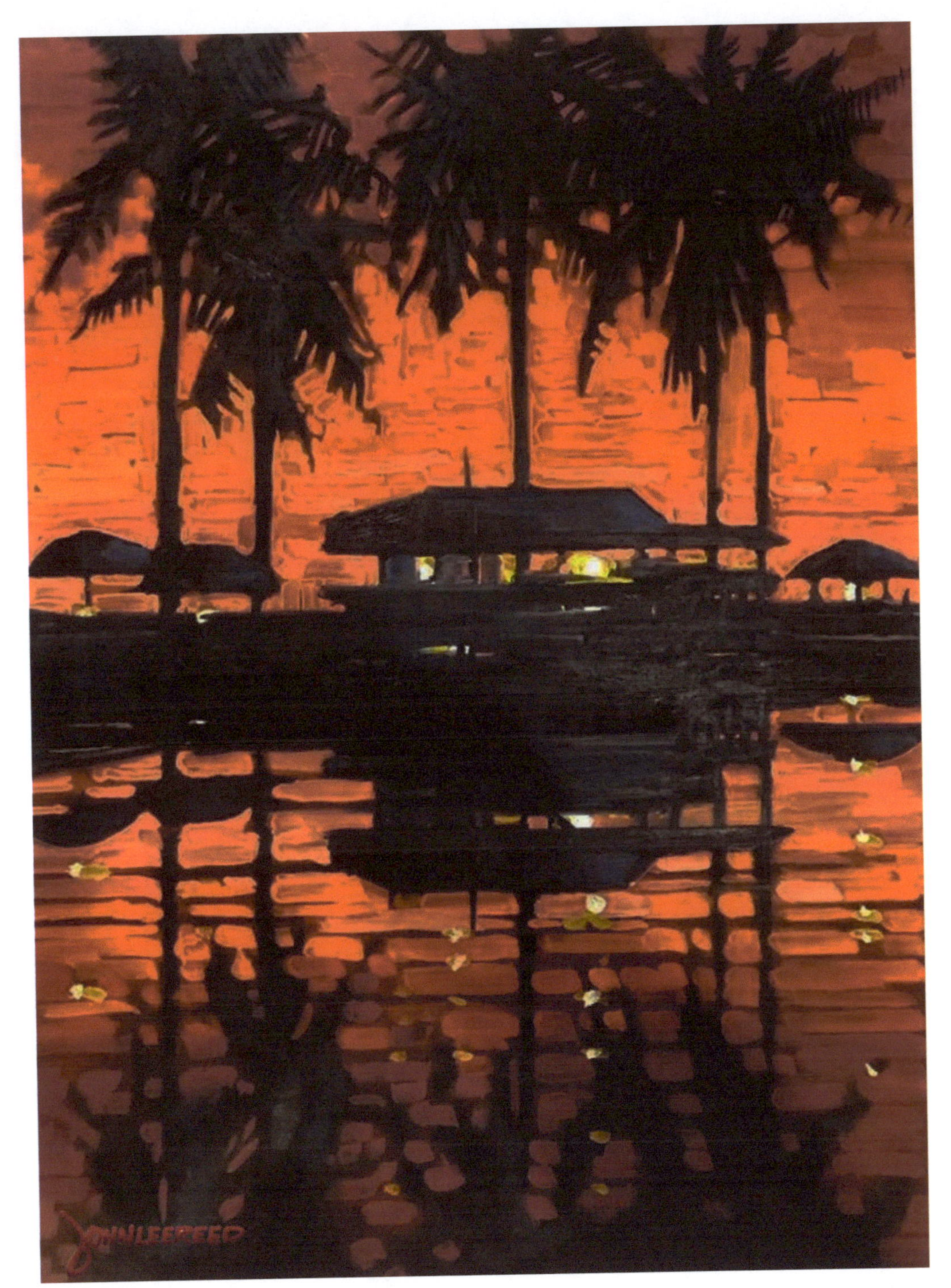

JOHNLEEREED

Notes